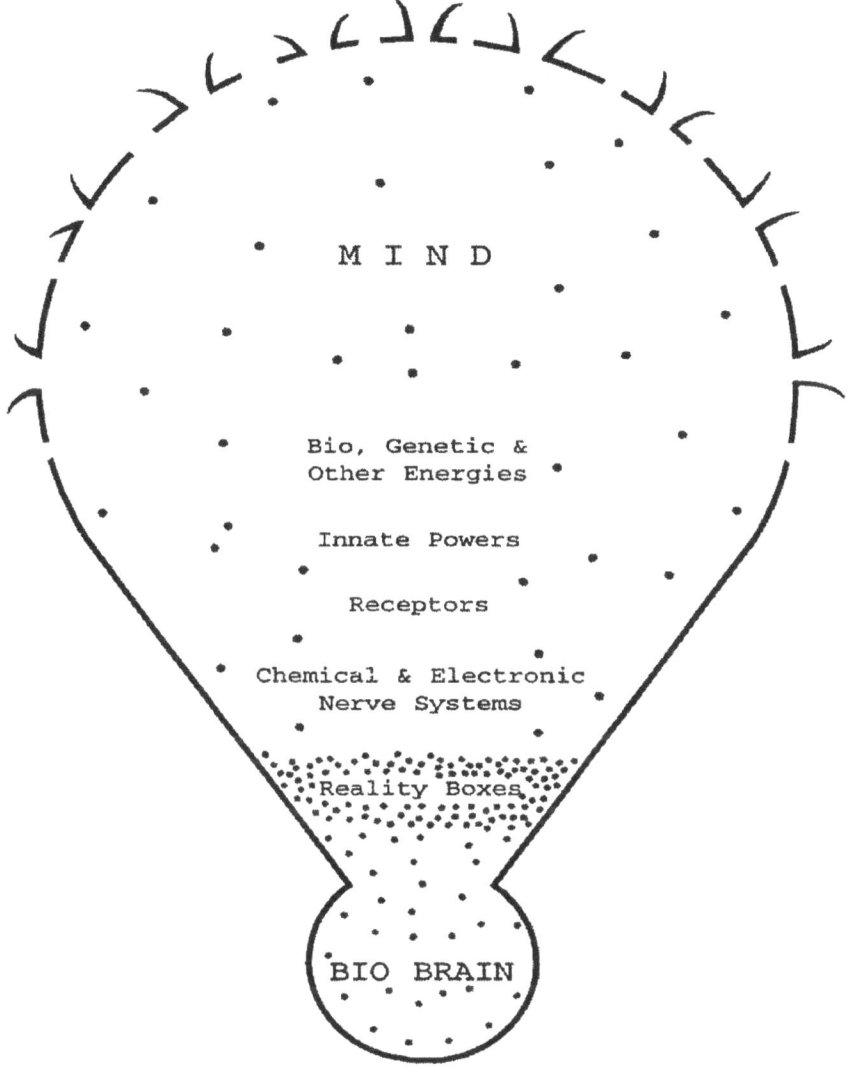

FRONTISPIECE. In discussing empowerment, it is to be accepted that we are dealing in MIND, or, more precisely, in mind stuffs and their remarkable activities. Thus, by extension, we are also dealing with components of mind, some of which are indicated in this diagram. MIND is not understood completely, and within limits of various societal forces many mind phenomena are denied the actuality they obviously deserve - for example, that minds and brains of individuals interact at levels and in ways other than the physical.

Ingo Swann (1933-2013) was an American artist and exceptionally successful subject in parapsychology experiments. As a child he spontaneously had numerous paranormal experiences, mostly of the OBE type, the future study of which became a major passion as he matured. In 1970, he began acting as a parapsychology test subject in tightly controlled laboratory settings with numerous scientific researchers. Because of the success of most of these thousands of test trials, major media worldwide often referred to him as "the scientific psychic." His subsequent research on behalf of American intelligence interests, including that of the CIA, won him top PSI-spy status.

His involvement in government research projects required the discovery of innovative approaches toward the actual realizing of subtle human energies. He viewed PSI powers as only parts of the larger spectrum of human sensing systems and was internationally known as an advocate and researcher of the exceptional powers of the human mind.

To learn more about Ingo, his work, art, and other books, please visit:

www.ingoswann.com

SECRETS OF POWER
VOLUME II

The Vitalizing of Individual Powers

A BioMind Superpowers Book
Published by

Swann-Ryder Productions, LLC
www.ingoswann.com

Copyright © 2002 by Ingo Swann; Copyright © 2015 by Murleen S. Ryder; Copyright © 2017 by Swann-Ryder Productions, LLC.

All rights reserved. No part of this book may be used or reproduced in any manner whatsoever without written permission.
For more information address: www.ingoswann.com.

Previously published in trade paperback by Ingo Swann Books and digitally by Crossroad Press.

First edition BioMind Superpowers Books.

Cover art: *Energy* by Ingo Swann © Swann-Ryder Productions, LLC.

ISBN-13: 978-1-949214-62-8

SECRETS OF POWER

VOLUME II

Ingo Swann

Experience is not what happens to a man, it is what a man does with what happens to him.
(Aldous Huxley)

Many are stubborn in pursuit of the path they have chosen, few in pursuit of the goal.
(Friedrich Nietzsche)

The more intelligent a man is, the more originality he discovers in men. Ordinary people see no difference between men.
(Blaise Pascal)

As a rule, I always look for what others ignore.
(Marshall McLuhan)

Talent is like electricity. We don't understand electricity. We use it.
(Maya Angelou)

CONSCIOUSNESS OF OUR POWERS AUGMENTS THEM.
(Marquis de Vauvenargues)

There are plenty of people to whom the crucial problems of their lives never get presented in terms they can understand.
(John Jay Chapman)

Everybody wants to be somebody: nobody wants to grow.
(Johann Wolfgang von Goethe)

The tragedy of life is not so much what men suffer, but rather what they miss.
(Thomas Carlyle)

Those who do not feel pain seldom think that it is felt.
(Dr. Samuel Johnson)

Man is a sun; and the senses are his planets.
(Baron Friedrich von Novalis)

One's real life is often the life that one does not lead.
(Oscar Wilde)

Where is your Self to be found? Always in the deepest enchantment that you have experienced.
(Hugo von Hofmannsthal)

This book is dedicated to the reality that all individuals of our human species are innate carriers of excellent powers, forms of intelligence, and superlative sensing systems.

Contents

Author's Notes x

Part One: Novel Overviews Relevant to Empowerment 1

Chapter 1: BIGGER PICTURES AND MISSING DEFINITIONS 2

Chapter 2: VERSIONS OF POWER AND EMPOWERMENT 8

Chapter 3: REALITY BOXES AND EMPOWERMENT MAPS 16

Chapter 4: THREE MAJOR CATEGORIES OF EMPOWERMENT AND POWER 21

Chapter 5: THE VITALIZATION OF EMPOWERMENT 24

Chapter 6: RECOGNITION OF EMPOWERMENT PROCESSES 26

Chapter 7: THE SPECTRUM OF HUMAN POWERS 31

Part Two: Unidentified Parts of Mind 35

Chapter 8: MAPS OF THE MIND 36

Chapter 9: THE ON-GOING CONFUSION OF POWERS-MIND-INTELLIGENCE 38

Chapter 10: THE PROBLEM OF KNOWING WHAT INTELLIGENCE IS 44

Chapter 11: ENERGIES OF MIND 50

Chapter 12: THE SUBCONSCIOUS PART OF MIND 52

Chapter 13: THE CONSCIOUS PART OF MIND AND ITS SURFACE ENERGIES 56

Chapter 14: THE STRENGTH-OF-POWER(S) PART OF MIND 59

Chapter 15: THE POWER NUCLEUS PART OF MIND 61

Part Three: Possible Routes for Entering Empowerment at the Individual Level 67

Chapter 16: EMPOWERMENT VIA REALITY BOX RETOOLING 68

Chapter 17: EMPOWERMENT VIA THE STUDY OF DEPOWERMENT 70

Chapter 18: EMPOWERMENT VIA THE PRINCIPLE OF UNFOLDMENT _____ 73

Chapter 19: EMPOWERMENT VIA ENHANCING HUMAN SENSES AND PERCEPTION ____ 77

Part Four: All Individuals Have Recognizable Innate Base Power Systems _____ 83

Chapter 20: THE REAL EXISTENCE OF POWER FACTORS _____ 84

Chapter 21: EACH HUMAN INDIVIDUAL IS EXTENSIVELY WIRED WITH INFORMATION RECEPTORS _____ 89

Chapter 22: EVERYONE HAS AT LEAST TWO INNATE SENSING SYSTEMS _____ 96

Chapter 23: THE "ELECTRO-IMPULSE" BASIS OF PERCEPTOR AND DETECTOR INFORMATION SYSTEMS _____ 103

Chapter 24: HUMAN POWERS EMPATHIC _____ 108

Chapter 25: HUMAN POWERS TELEPATHIC _____ 114

Chapter 26: HUMAN POWERS OF OBSERVING _____ 119

Chapter 27: HUMAN AWARE POWERS _____ 122

Chapter 28: HUMAN ATTENTION POWERS _____ 124

Chapter 29: HUMAN PROJECTING POWERS _____ 127

Part Five: The Real Existence of Human Groking Powers _____ 131

Chapter 30: GETTING BEYOND LIMITATIONS OF REALITY BOXES AND LANGUAGE SYSTEMS _____ 132

Chapter 31: HUMAN POWERS OF GROKING SIGNIFICANCE AND IMPORTANCE _____ 138

Chapter 32: HUMAN GROKING POWERS OF EXPERIENCING _____ 141

Chapter 33: HUMAN GROKING POWERS OF COGNIZING _____ 144

Chapter 34: HUMAN GROKING POWERS OF SOURCING FROM BEYOND-SELF _____ 148

Ingo Swann

AUTHOR'S NOTES

POWER UNFOLDMENT at the individual level is probably one of the most spectacular of all human phenomena.

We can say this at least hypothetically -- because we know that individuals innately have more powers than those few permitted by various societal formats and the empowerment power restrictions in them.

It is because of such restrictors that we do not often witness spectacular individual power unfoldment per se.

What we usually see instead is just enough unfoldment of individual personas so as to fit them, one way or another, into various slots within their social and societal environments. And as discussed throughout Volume I of this series, those social and societal environments in fact determine what power is to be or not to be. And it is thus power that tends to be understood only within the contexts of social power games, while innate human powers are seldom understood if at all.

If the foregoing is considered as calmly as possible, it can then be seen that the human is a social creature as well as an individual, and that where the one leaves off and the other begins is quite difficult to determine. And so there are difficulties establishing what The Individual actually is.

The concept of The Individual is, of course, quite precious and meaningful, and especially so within the philosophical systems of the highly developed countries of the modern West.

But it is fair to point out that the concept of an individualistic persona, and the philosophy of individualism as such, did not really achieve formal description until the nineteenth century. Up until then, the term INDIVIDUAL generally applied only to separate things within a given group or category.

◻

In the early 1830s, the French politician and writer, Alexis de Tocqueville (1805-1859) undertook a government mission to the United States to study penal systems. But he studied American politics and behavior, too.

These studies resulted in his famous book DEMOCRACY IN AMERICA (1835), in which, among other things, he indicated that "Individualism is a novel [American] expression to which a novel idea has given birth. Individualism is a mature and calm feeling, which disposes each member of the community to sever himself from the mass of his fellow creatures and to draw apart with his family and friends."

This "novel idea" caught on like a wildfire and was soon given more terse definition as: "Self-centered feeling or conduct as a principle; a mode of life in which the individual pursues his own ends or follows his own ideas; free and independent individual action or thought; egoism."

By 1870, INDIVIDUALISM had even achieved, of all things, a metaphysical definition: "The doctrine that the individual is a self-determined whole, and that any larger whole is merely an aggregate of individuals, which, if they act on each other at all, do so externally."

By 1884, the term had been given an additional definition as "The social theory which advocates the free and independent action of the individual as opposed to communistic methods of organization and state interference."

Meanwhile, earlier in about 1840, the term INDIVIDUALIST had come into general usage and was defined as: "One who pursues an independent or egoistic course in thought or action."

Needless to say, individualists are easier to recognize than are the many nuances of individualism that usually have diverse complications and gray areas surrounding them.

These definitions, all formulated during the nineteenth century, have been provided here for what they are worth in general.

They continue to seem sensible enough at first take. But the concepts they initially established have proven to be quite superficial, and so there has been little agreement among subsequent authorities as to what the individual consists of.

One of the on-going problems that seems to be involved is quite similar to one that plagues concepts of empowerment at the individual level. Certain concepts can be functional within a given level of reality, but not in others.

Another way of stating this is that certain concepts can be real enough in various mind-sets or given reality boxes but have lesser or no meaning in others.

It is this multiplicity of levels of reality, mind-sets, and reality boxes that complicates the contexts of empowerment, and those of power itself -- for, as many come to realize, or perhaps experience to their surprise -- empowerment and power can be achieved within certain contexts but can fall flat in others.

This is to emphasize that given ideas of The Individual, of empowerment, and about power emanate from the mind-sets or reality boxes that produce them. And, as most can realize, what works for a given reality box can be ineffective, meaningless, and sterile with respect to others.

◻

There is one possible reason it has proven so difficult to establish conclusive definitions about what The Individual consists of.

This is that The Individual is the reality box in which The Individual is dwelling at any given time, and out of which is produced The Individual's thoughts and actions -- and also, it may as well be said, The Individual's operative survival ratio into the future.

If all reality boxes were the same in clone-like accord, and always remained that way through the generations, then what individuals consist of could be defined with some precision -- and, as well, their thoughts and actions could efficiently be predicted.

Indeed, elements of this kind of thing can easily be identified in the reality-box conditioning practices of most societal power structures. In those structures, the less powerful and the powerless are supposed to exist in clone-like accord as determined by the power structure, whether it is large or small.

From this kind of thing, it can be concluded, in a larger-picture way, that societal power structures can initiate and maintain reality-box cloning.

Well, yes.

◻

But there is an even larger picture. For, as is understood, and as our history demonstrates, the reality boxes of this and that societal power structure come and go -- to be REPLACED by new and other ones requiring new and other reality-box cloning practices.

If this is contemplated upon as serenely as possible, there is only ONE WAY that such multiple reality-box transitions can occur.

While it IS the case that societal power structures can initiate this or that reality-box cloning and management, it is the HUMAN SPECIES that has the generic and innate power to manufacture reality boxes of ANY kind.

After all, wheresoever humans are or go, there also will be found reality boxes of this or that kind, and nowhere can be found a human that is entirely reality-boxless.

◻

In that this is so, it is the better part of valor to assume that whatever the species has downloads into each and all specimens of it. It is thus that we find all individuals have reality boxes, whether of the tattered or highly organized kind.

Because of the magnitude involved, the innate species power of manufacturing reality boxes is a wondrous thing -- the direct implication being that there are no real or even illusory realities that permanently fall outside of possible or potential cognizance.

It can be understood, however, that possible or potential cognizance on such a scale is something that is problematical to most power structures -- whose stability much depends upon not too much cognizance outside of whatever cognizance is permissible.

Secrets of Power (II)

One of the bottom lines of this small discussion is that there are two general perspectives regarding individual empowerment.

One can seek empowerment within the contexts of some kind of social or societal reality-box power games. This perspective is, of course, entirely recognizable.

One can seek empowerment within the contexts of human powers that are innate and contained in our species. This perspective is not very recognizable, because what human powers actually consist of falls into the category of forbidden knowledge.

With respect to this latter perspective (and as discussed throughout Volume I), the best way to preserve the pyramidal power structure format and the power status of the few, is to prevent information and knowledge about power, human powers, and empowerment from accumulating and becoming accessible to all individuals who might benefit from it.

It is thus, even in our present age of information gluts, that there are no socially endorsed power schools or encyclopedias that reveal in-depth information about power and all that can be associated with it.

These absences are particularly noticeable within the modern age of so-called universal enlightenment, and which, to be sure, has produced encyclopedic knowledge sources for just about everything else.

The traditional concept most central to the long-enduring pyramidal power structure arrangement holds that the majority of individuals are born innately inferior to those who are born innately superior to them, especially with respect to intelligence. The many sad and revolting implications of this long-enduring concept have been discussed in Volume I of this series -- and, as well, in a recent book entitled THE MAKING OF INTELLIGENCE, by Ken Richardson (Weidenfeld & Nicolson, London, 1999), herewith highly recommended to anyone seriously interested in individual empowerment.

Any enlightened discussion of the revolting traditional concept brings into view a very important, two-part question regarding individual empowerment: whether most, or even some, individuals are naturally born without innate powers; or whether, via the processes of social conditioning, individuals are rendered ignorant of their innate powers, an ignorance that works to diminish those innate powers into inactive states.

At least part of an answer here is that it is difficult to see how individuals can function at all unless they are born with an innate spectrum of powers, a spectrum that, furthermore, is quite extensive as will be considered in the text ahead.

Just because a large number of those powers can be rendered non-operational by social conditioning should not be taken as proof-positive that a spectrum of innate powers does not exist in each individual.

This author posits and accepts that all individuals born of our species ARE born with a rather large spectrum of innate powers -- especially that of mind-intelligence and which requires the support of several subsidiary kinds of powers.

But it is also posited that few realize what the fuller spectrum of their powers are because there is no place one can consult in order to find out what they are. And the continuing absence of detailed encyclopedias about human powers will ensure the perpetuation of this particular kind of non-knowledge.

While there are no encyclopedias that specialize in describing human power phenomena, it can be discovered that many earlier dictionaries identify and define numerous powers. The two dictionaries this author majorly depends on are Webster's Seventh New Collegiate Dictionary (1974), and the much more extensive Oxford Dictionary of the English Language. Other sources consulted are identified in the text.

It is difficult to surmise what individuals think power consists of. But the evidence is very good that many identify power and empowerment within this or that social context -- the home, the local environment, various peer groupings, the workplace, various economic workings, the career industries, the ever-changing political and professional competitions, and etc.

It is of course important to learn how to better survive and function within social contexts, and so there is nothing intrinsically amiss with such aims.

But there are important distinctions to be made between social context empowerment and the contexts of innate human powers in general. And in fact, it can be discerned or intuited that recognition and enhancement of one's own innate powers can magnify one's empowerment in social contexts.

Beyond the individual, group, social, and cultural levels is the much bigger picture of the human species itself.

If the species level is considered, it can certainly be understood that all power and empowerment activities, no matter where, when, or to what degree, are manifestations within the overall species context.

In that context, whatever individuals are or become, they are first and foremost members, or life units, which are downloaded from within the proliferating species out of which they have descended.

The contents of this volume are thus based on the observable fact that the human species possesses a large range of powers, and that these, in formative essence, download into each individual born of the species.

At least some of these powers are so innately basic that no individual can achieve any kind of operational or functional survival without them -- and it is a discussion of some of these basic powers, innately present in all individuals, which provide the principal contents of this volume.

A WORKING DEFINITION OF HUMAN POWERS IS BEST ESTABLISHED AS INNATE, INBORN SOURCES OF SUPPLYING ENERGY -- AND WHICH SOURCES ARE CAPABLE OF MAGNIFICATION, OF DECREASE, OF BEING LATENT AND UNTAPPED, AND OF BEING DE-ENERGIZED OR DEPOWERED.

Indeed, synonyms for POWER are usually given as force, energy, strength, and might. These synonyms reflect qualities of power that can be exerted physically and mentally -- all of which can be nurtured and enhanced or caused to be latent or weakened.

As with the issues discussed in Volume I, the topics selected for presentation in this volume can be identified and verified by those individuals interested in doing so.

A NOTE ABOUT THE SUGGESTED EXERCISES

ALTHOUGH MUCH is known about learning processes, there is still a lot that remains mysterious and unknown.

Even so, it is clear enough that the human mind is designed for learning. It is also obvious that social processes in which everyone is embedded greatly determine what we do and do not learn, and it is this factor that accounts for all types of failure to nurture many learning potentials.

One general factor that is not so obvious is that people best recognize what they expect to see and often fail in recognizing whatever they do not expect to see. This factor is well understood, for example, in the movie producing industry where statistics show that films that reflect expectations of the many are more likely to make more money.

This factor is closely related to another having to do with the fact that people not only see, but best sense and experience what they expect to, and have trouble sensing and experiencing what they do not expect. For example, most do not expect to experience telepathy or intuition or other subtle activities supporting empowerment. And so they might not realize that such activities go on all the time about them. Thus, what we expect to see is visible to us, while the unexpected can easily remain invisible.

Various studies about the processes of perception reveal two important issues. First, what we expect to see/experience has meaning, whereas what we do not expect can remain meaningless.

Second, the ratios involved with this are surprisingly high. It is not unusual to find that many live and experience exclusively within the socially conditioned norms of their expectations on a ratio that can range as high as 98 per cent. Much can be deduced from this.

For example, the socially engineered poor and powerless often do not expect significant increases in wealth and power, and so the subtle wherewithal of empowerment phenomena might remain invisible and meaningless even though empowerment potentials are innate within them.

With respect to learning, we learn best what we expect to learn, or what seems most meaningful to learn, and usually so only within the criteria of whatever social contexts we inhabit. And as discussed in Volume I of this series, most social contexts are power-competitive and so they do not nurture too much empowerment in too many.

In general, learning is principally assumed to consist of being taught something by others, and this is indeed the great workhorse of all educational processes, methods, and learning packages.

But sometimes there are bitter bottom lines to this. One of these is that learning is thought of as coming from outside of self, and it is via this factor that innate elements of awareness and perception naturally present within are diminished and not nurtured.

Another factor, perhaps more serious, is that others cannot teach what they, themselves, do not know about, and, in any event can only teach what coincides with their own reality boxes, awareness, and perception.

With regard to learning about power and empowerment, the overall situation is quite complex. As but one example of this complexity identified by the critic Julian Barnes, "books are where things are explained to you, life is where they are not, and I'm not surprised that some people prefer books."

One can think of power and empowerment as a life principle, not a book principle, for books can only reflect the reality boxes of their authors, and which, in the end, may not have too much to do with the ever-present, multiplex situation of realities behind realities behind other realities.

Explanatory books about power and empowerment are more than welcome. But power and empowerment go on in life more than in books, and so in addition to books one must also learn to look into life factors themselves.

No one can learn about, or deal with, what they are not aware of and hence do not perceive. But everyone learns from what they can become aware of and perceive. And the case is very good that the advent of new awareness and perception triggers activation of new responsive empowerment systems within.

One of the facts of life, where little is explained, is that it is populated with multitudes of other people, each of which displays not only a tangible, visible surface -- but ALSO a mind-dynamic interior which may or may not be all that visible or can be completely invisible altogether.

This is entirely compatible with the complexity of life itself, having both visible and invisible components -- and thus arise the many problems of what one may or may not become aware of and perceive.

There can be little doubt that individuals, as they are taught to do, first focus awareness and perception on the directly tangible, the physically obvious, and that incremental categories of learning do take place in this manner.

Indeed, we all learn much from others in this way, and our powers of awareness and perception increase accordingly.

However, as discussed in the text ahead, we all have reality boxes that, after strong formatting, might decrease awareness and perception of whatever does not fit into them -- especially with respect to more subtle, non-tangible factors at work in others and in life that is NOT organized in book form.

The suggested exercises in these volumes of SECRETS OF POWER point out factors that can be identified and confirmed as existing if an attempt is made to do so, and the recognition of which might increase awareness, perception, and empowerment potentials in one's own interior.

Some of these factors are easier to identify and perceive than others, and so patience and persistence might enter into whatever is involved.

All of the suggested exercises in these volumes are elective and they are useful only to the degree they turn out to be self-informative.

Where exercises are not suggested, the reader is invited to explore their own ways and means of increasing recognition first of life phenomena external to them, and then perhaps discovering innate factors in themselves predesigned to deal and interact with such life phenomena.

PART ONE
NOVEL OVERVIEWS RELEVANT TO EMPOWERMENT

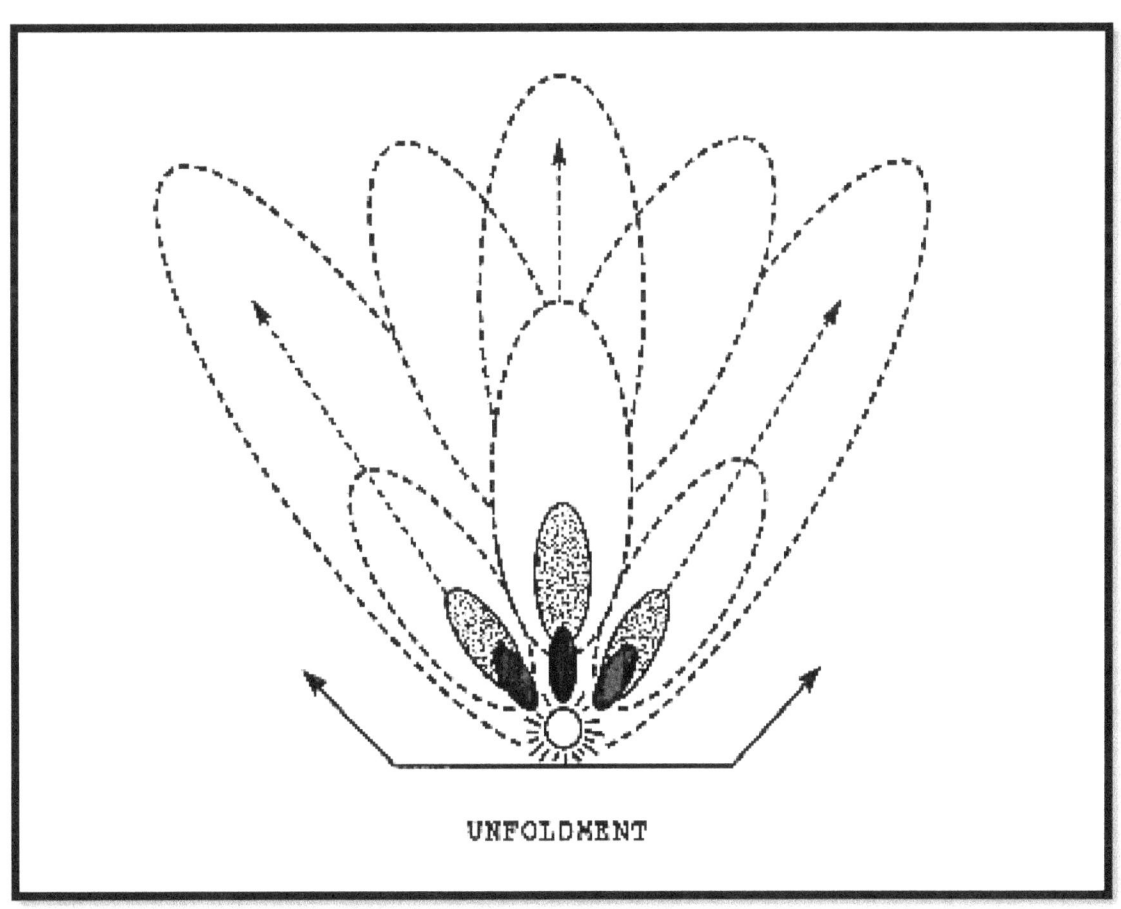

UNFOLDMENT

Chapter 1

BIGGER PICTURES AND MISSING DEFINITIONS

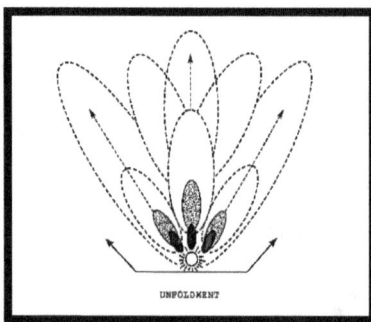

IF POWER was not considered a very precious thing, then no one would care if empowerment was possible or not, and anyone could indulge in empowerment studies and activities without interference.

But power IS considered a precious possession, and hence it is broadly treated as are all precious things.

ANY access to it is jealously guarded and thwarted via very serious competitions -- and this not just by the powerful, but also by a wide selection of others in all walks of life preferring empowerment for themselves rather than for someone else.

It follows that anyone showing symptoms of empowerment comes under close observation by many, and thus begins the long tale of conflict of depowerment versus empowerment, many particulars of which have been discussed in Volume I.

THE AMAZING ABSENCE OF CERTAIN IMPORTANT DEFINITIONS

One of the results of this long-enduring and ever-continuing conflict is that we have no meaningful definition of empowerment. The term is minimalized even in dictionaries -- a fact that can be confirmed by anyone taking the time to do so.

There are, however, two standard dictionary definitions for POWER, the first and most familiar of which is given as: "Possession of control, authority, or influence over others" -- with emphasis, of course, on POSSESSION of such.

The second definition, which is omitted from some contemporary dictionaries, is given as: "A particular active property, capacity, or faculty of body or mind."

It is understood that the "particular active property" somehow leads into "Ability to act or affect something strongly; to physical or mental force; to might, vigor, and energy; to force of character."

While the foregoing definitions seem decent and clear enough, the second one at least is actually ambiguous in the extreme because the "particular active property" is not attributed to anything at all, and one is therefore left in ignorance about its formative essence.

The term ABILITY is often thought of as synonymous with POWER, but it is not -- if definitions are to be adhered to.

The pertinent definition of ABILITY is given as "Acquired competence in doing, skill, aptitude, proficiency; and natural talent (perhaps)."

There is a rather large distance between "particular active property" and "acquired competence," a distance that leads to the question as to how and by what means the "competence" can come into existence.

Surely, if the "particular active property" is, shall we say, not all that active, then it is dubious that it can affect anything -- a situation that we can now see equates to various kinds of powerlessness.

If one has attentively been following the foregoing discussion, it can become apparent that there is no descriptive definition for the "particular active property."

The absence of such a definition is quite amazing, in that the particular active property is assumed to exist behind whatever affects it causes, and which affects are in no way small matters of importance.

In respect to this omission, it becomes possible to wonder if the "particular active property" could exist if human powers did not.

And if one elects to wonder about this, one might as well also wonder if there is a well-considered definition regarding the essential nature of human powers -- the answer to which is once more mostly in the negative.

By now it might have become clear that some working definitions need to be provided to fill in for some absent ones, at least for the contexts of this book.

A tentative working definition on behalf of human powers might be thought of as referring to those powers that are:

INNATE, INBORN SOURCES OF SUPPLYING ENERGY -- AND WHICH SOURCES ARE CAPABLE OF ENHANCEMENT, OF MAGNIFICATION, OF DECREASE, OF BEING LATENT AND UNTAPPED, AND OF BEING DEENERGIZED OR DEPOWERED.

Indeed, synonyms for POWER are usually given as force, energy, strength, and might.

These synonyms reflect qualities of power that can be exerted physically and mentally -- all of which can be nurtured, enhanced, (i.e., empowered), or caused to be latent or weakened (i.e., depowered.)

If it becomes possible to begin appreciating the large extent of human powers at the species level, it can easily be thought that our species is a power species in essence, activity, productivity, and mental dynamism.

In that sense, it can also be thought that the human mind is a vehicle for objectifying the innate powers, the sum of which denotes the extensive scope of the "human potential," and which, so far as yet known, distinguishes the human life form from all other known life forms on the planet Earth.

HUMANS ARE OVER-ENDOWED WITH POWERS THEY DON'T USE

If even partially appreciated, the large extent of identifiable human powers at the species level clearly points up the fact that our species is over-endowed with respect to survival at the animal level.

Indeed, our species does not need so many powers in order to merely survive, and many of the powers are in fact surplus with respect to the goal of mere physical survival.

This brings up the question as to why the human species life form should be over-endowed with a surplus of innate powers not really needed for mere biological survival in terrestrial environments.

It might seem, then, that the human power species is more designed to exist or coexist with respect to other species that are mind-dynamically equivalent to our own - and in which case our species' powers might not constitute a strange surplus, but a primal and appropriate necessity.

In the past, many thinkers and researchers have attempted to place the human species within terrestrial contexts having to do with other formative bio-species therein, and with whatever paleoanthropic "record" can be discovered.

This seems a logical process to undertake, and it is, to a certain degree. But, as many critics have noted, that process always requires various kinds of reductionism that can seem meaningful only if the full species-spectrum of human powers is minimalized, avoided, or truncated.

If the full species-spectrum of human powers would be admitted into evidence, then the human species more or less stands forth as entirely out of place within all recognizable terrestrial contexts.

After all, the human species is the only one we know of that not only constructs but also destroys civilizations, this apparently a result of that "particular active property" that remains undefined.

THE HUMAN POWER SPECIES

If a species IS a power species, then the playing of power games would be one of its principal hallmarks.

Here one is talking not only of the physical survival of the strongest and fittest, but of the survival of the most stealthy and clever, and of those who manage to obtain active power over the developmental empowerment potentials of others.

One sardonic estimate of our human power species is that a rather large proportion of its generations of individuals wish more than anything else to belong to and survive within the contexts of power games (large or small).

And so it can at least be observed that a significant proportion of individuals of our species not only live and breathe power games, but judge their survival success almost exclusively within power games contexts -- and often to the detriment of other contexts.

If a power species existed in relationship to some other power species, then to survive, it would have to nurture and enhance its innate powers and externalize them with respect to the power games of other power species.

This enhancement process would require enhancing its innate powers with the qualities of force, energy, strength, might, and excellent dynamisms.

But if a power species was isolated from other power species, then the odds are that it would introvert its power games within the contexts of its own species.

This, of course, is the same as saying that the isolated power species would play competitive power games within itself -- meaning among all of the individuals that comprise the species at any given time.

Something like this of course constitutes the history of our species within the limits of terrestrial contexts. Indeed, human history, so-called, provides the best evidence that the human species is a power species having the demonstrated credentials as such.

It should be mentioned, without going into it too deeply, that as long as a power species remains isolated from others, its history of intra-competitive powers games can be extended, without much pause, into its future.

Our human power species is clearly isolated in terrestrial terms. But the advent of the real possibility of other "advanced intelligence" species elsewhere in the cosmos made its appearance in the last half of the twentieth century.

It is already broadly assumed that "We are not alone," as it is put, even though the implications, facts, and knowledge involved are cloaked in serious and nervous secrecy and cover-ups.

THE SUPPRESSION OF HUMAN POWERS ON BEHALF OF HUMAN POWER GAMES

Meanwhile, back at our isolated terrestrial ranch, our power species plays power games within itself, and one clearly identified game is to achieve power over the empowerment of others.

As we know, this particular game results in the control, influence, and authority by the successful few over the others less or not successful at it - and who are collectively referred to as the powerless.

The best method, having many tested historical precedents, for achieving power over the others is to keep knowledge and information about power, human powers, and empowerment as unavailable as possible.

As discussed in Volume I of this series, this activity, on-going over time, has brought into existence a rather enormous covert depowerment industry, the principal machinations of which are so clever and subtle that few realize it exists -- or can accept that it does.

Even so, if human powers innate at the species level can constitute a first bigger picture, the enormous covert depowerment industry is without any doubt the second.

In the contexts of those two bigger pictures, then, the picture of THE INDIVIDUAL is clearly rather small, even if individuality is considered as having special importance. Thus arises something akin to an enigma or a conundrum, an intricate problem that can be described as follows.

Each individual of our species is a carrier of human powers and is therefore not only important but also valuable.

However, the large majority of individuals are rather meaningless within the context of power games and the ongoing depowerment industry. They are also victimized and extensively wasted on behalf of those games, in the form of large and senseless body counts and the societal deadening of their innate powers.

Because of this conundrum, there are distinctions to be made between (1) empowerment within the contexts of power games and the depowerment industry, and (2) human empowerment overall.

It can easily be seen that (1) above will ultimately exclude most individuals, and that (2) can include all individuals.

However, (2) above has something to do with not only defeating the on-going machinations of the power games depowerment industry, but also with transcending its many versions at least in vision and awareness.

As has been discussed in Volume I, empowerment of any kind is made difficult by the total absence of encyclopedias about power, and especially about the nature and existence of human powers overall.

This crucial absence ensures the continuation of general ignorance of knowledge about human powers in general. It also occludes general awareness about how many of them there are.

The most probable reason as to why there is no encyclopedia of human powers was pointed up (in 1746) by the Marquis de Vauvenargues, the French moralist and epigrammatist, who indicated "Consciousness of our powers augments them."

This can be rephrased to read: "Becoming conscious of our powers starts up their activation."

Can empowerment be as simple as that? Perhaps not. But in the gross absence of information and knowledge about our powers, becoming conscious of them is a good place to start.

SUGGESTED RESEARCH

IN A KINDLY AND INTERESTED MANNER ASK NUMEROUS INDIVIDUALS WHAT THEY THINK EMPOWERMENT CONSISTS OF THIS IS MERELY A DISCOVERY PROCESS SO DO NOT ARGUE ANY ISSUES, AND BE PREPARED AS WELL FOR SOME SURPRISES

Chapter 2

VERSIONS OF POWER AND EMPOWERMENT

```
       FIXED
        SET
   PRESCRIBED
    DETERMINED
     PERSISTENT
      OBSTINATE
      IMMOVABLE
        RIGID
RELUCTANT TO CHANGE
```

THERE ARE many versions of power, and so there will also be many ideas, whether real or imagined, about empowerment.

Thus, the worldwide panorama of power and empowerment is altogether composed of an abundance of contrasting concepts and vast heaps of different kinds of information.

The whole of this is packed with endless confusions and contortions, the totality of which is very difficult to deal with.

Even so, there ARE three factors within the confusing morass that are certain, permanent, and unarguable:

A. THAT human powers do exist within our species, and thus within each and every one;
B. THAT mind and its parts are involved;
C. THAT reality boxes also exist, and which largely determine how and if (A) and (B) are understood.

AS already mentioned, among many other gems of thought, the French writer Luc de Vauvenargues (1715-1747) indicated that becoming conscious of our powers augments them -- AUGMENT meaning, of course, "to enlarge or increase, especially in size, amount, or degree."

In this, he illuminated the distinction between being conscious or non-conscious of our powers at the group and individual levels -- the direct implication being that remaining non-conscious of our powers does not augment them.

Indeed, one usually cannot deal or work with whatever one is non-conscious of. And so, in any first instance of empowerment, one must become conscious of what one's innate powers actually are.

In a larger and more encompassing reality, one must also become consciously aware of (B) and (C) above -- PLUS one other all-important factor.

This is the factor of social and societal control not only of power, but also of empowerment itself.

As discussed at length in Volume I, within societal power structures, power and empowerment are considered very -- precious and highly competitive commodities, and so easy access to them is very carefully and jealously guarded via endless open and secret tricks of the power crafts, fair or foul.

Like it or not, this is one of the major facts of human life.

As most realize, the very many versions of power and empowerment can be found along a scale ranging from the stupid to the enlightened, with real and/or empty configurations in between.

Even so, any given version of power is likely to attract adherents to it, somewhat along the lines implied by the old saying that "birds of a feather flock together."

One of the everlasting detriments of this kind of thing is that a given format of power can become more important than the individuals emotionally and intellectually incorporated within it -- with the result that over time the individuals themselves, much to their surprise, can be victimized by the format.

This possibility is not generally noticed at first when a power format is on the upswing. When the power format fails, its adherents can become power "homeless," sometimes even in tragic and terminal ways.

Indeed, history is replete with the dramatics and sagas of the rise and fall of power formats, especially during the twentieth century still fresh in collective memory.

Although this can be interpreted as being rather depressing, it is meaningful regarding the contents and objectives of this volume, which have to do with the more happy and exciting prospect of empowerment of the individual as such,

The foregoing scenario brings into question what the individual actually is with respect to power and empowerment.

And, if history can be relied upon, any societal power format is clearly a temporary one -- whether shorter or longer -- not only with respect to on-going time, but also with respect to ongoing testing via familiar power competitions.

The two points made above signify something that is hardly ever brought to light -- that it is far easier to achieve a guise of empowerment within the contexts of some kind power format one might enter into than it is to empower self as a discrete individual.

HYPNOTIC QUALITIES OF POWER

There is yet another aspect that can be added to the first two mentioned above. Many have probably become aware of this aspect, even though it tends not to be openly discussed.

There are a number of topics that overall exude certain hypnotic qualities on a big-time scale -- and power, of course, is almost certainly the preeminent of these. Other such topics are sex, money, betrayal, destruction, and, not the least of them, mind-control.

Why, exactly, those topics have the hypnoid-like fascination and allure they do is open for further discussion.

Certainly, one can realize that they are powerful elements, especially when dynamically used in combined formulas for fiction and moviemaking.

And it is certainly quite apparent that those topics are strategically important to most formats of power managing entrepreneurship having to do with authority, influence, and control over others.

The purpose here for mentioning the real existence of such hypnotic qualities having "high energy" is that many other human qualities cannot hold a candle to them.

For example, the qualities of positive creativity and enlightenment, and especially of enlightened power, are considered deadbeats against the "power" of the more hypnotic qualities.

The reason for mentioning the hypnotic qualities at this point has again to do with how the individual, as such, can be considered or defined.

Those hypnotic qualities evoke mass and massive responses among our species as a whole, whether as adjuncts of power or not. It is certain that most might interpret, in some full part, their relationships with others via some choice among those qualities.

But, with some exceptions, those qualities are obviously downloaded from some kind of mass consciousness -- against which the concept of the individual becomes at least somewhat blurred.

Indeed, some formats of power seem deliberately to blur the issues involved, largely because a blurred "individual" consciousness is more responsive to power controls.

SELF-POWER IS INCORPORATED IN THE HUMAN SPECIES GENOME

While the foregoing discussions involve rather tough issues, the issue of "individual empowerment" IS a tough one.

If it were otherwise, then more individuals would succeed in individual empowerment. And this, in turn, has to do with the selection of self-power topics discussed in this volume.

Although most do not pay much attention to the fact, our human species actually comprises a wondrous and awesome genome of bio body, mind, energies, and innate powers.

Indeed, as already mentioned, our species as a whole possesses powers far in excess of those ordinarily used or are nurtured into functional activity.

This clearly means that our species is, of all things, over-endowed with regard to mere physical survival on the planet Earth.

While it is accepted that each individual downloads from the combined genes of a mother and a father, in better actuality all humans download from our species genome, which is abundantly equipped with powers of all kinds.

This is then to acknowledge that each individual is a specimen of our species -- and that each specimen somehow carries a working copy of the genome itself.

If this were NOT the case, the genome could not reproduce itself via born individuals, and the species based on the genome would become extinct.

After birth, and at the species level, the individual is expected to survive in the genome sense, for otherwise the individual need not be born.

Since recorded antiquity, all factors that assist in or equate to this survival have always been referred to as powers, or via equivalent terms in different languages.

Our present concept of powers has lost a very important nuance that used to be incorporated in earlier times.

In English, this lost nuance is reflected by the definitions of DYNAMIC and ENERGETIC.

And, indeed, a power that does not become dynamic and energetic is a useless one -- even though there is a latent copy for it in the genetic background of each individual.

If the abundance of human powers does not automatically suggest as much, this species-wide, heritable dynamism trait is surely one of the first clues that our species is a fully equipped power species and is MEANT as one by the genome itself.

Beyond the foregoing considerations, our species is a collectivizing social one, and so what is considered as survival ends up depending on whatever the reality boxes of different social arrangements and orders see and ordain as such.

REALITY BOXES

One now wonders what a reality box consists of. The phrase is actually of rather recent vintage, coming into increasing usage only during the last fifty years of the twentieth century.

But there is earlier precedent for the idea of the reality box.

For example, the remarkable English artist and poet William Blake (1757-1827), pointed up the following in his book THE MARRIAGE OF HEAVEN AND HELL (1790):

"If the doors of perception were cleansed, everything would appear to man as it is, infinite. [But] man has closed himself up till he sees all [only] thro' narrow chinks of his own cavern."

This "cavern," to be sure, equates to what today can easily be called a reality box -- with the possible emendation that some reality boxes don't have too many "chinks" or have none at all.

In any event, the existence of reality boxes is real. Everyone has them, and so in one sense at least, the prospect of empowerment can be considered a battle of reality boxes. This includes one's own, as well as all others of them.

As is commonly understood, social orders quickly erect generic formats of power structures, which can properly be referred to as societal reality boxes.

Any in-depth examination of power therefore has two options.

An examination of the important aspects regarding the distribution of societal power within typical power structures, which has been undertaken in Volume I.

And thenceforth an examination (in this Volume II) of the fundamental powers innate within our species, copies of which are encoded into each individual, whether or not each realizes as much.

That individuals might not realize the full scope of their innate powers is, in some absolute sense, NOT their fault. The fault is with the societal phenomena regarding the always-unequal distribution of collective power outlined in Volume I.

REALITY BOXES vs SELF-POWER

Almost everyone appreciates the fact that individuals are comprised of biophysical bodies each of which is separate from all others.

This individual separateness is seen as very precious, and so it is extended to include the minds of individuals, each of which is then assumed to be individually separate from all others.

But when individual minds begin to share and adapt to given information packages and frames of reference, they become copy-like or clone-like with each other.

Additionally, adaptation to information packages and frames of reference produces the contours and boundaries of mental reality boxes, the inner workings of which are limited to whatever information frames of reference have formatted the boxes.

Each individual, therefore, is not only a separate biophysical body, but is also a walking, talking, reality box having frames of reference that might not be as individual as one might think.

There are three very good reasons for addressing these issues before entering into the text ahead.

Reality boxes that are mentally shared make it largely possible to categorize and compartmentalize individuals into various groups, into various social strata and echelons, and into various levels of meaningful or non-meaningful empowered or depowered status.

Here is one of the most important make/break points with respect to empowerment and power.

For some decades now, it has been understood that the first of the fundamental frames of reference that are basic to reality boxes are formatted and undergo bio-mental lockdown at about the age of seven -- when the physical biobody undergoes very powerful glandular changes in preparation for forthcoming physical and mental maturation.

Thereafter, additional frames of reference can be incorporated, but usually only if they are more or less consistent with those that have already undergone lockdown. Additionally, the lockdown will lock out information and frames of reference that are not consistent.

Whenever frames of reference are acquired, mentally duplicated, and looked in, they tend to subside into the subconscious wherein they "work" in some sort of autonomic way that is not yet completely understood.

The whole of this kind of thing then constitutes how reality boxes become SET -- "set" in this case meaning "settled, fixed, prescribed, determined, persistent, reluctant to change, obstinate, immovable, and rigid."

Although the four points discussed above might be difficult to format in one's mind, it is common experience that one can look around and easily recognize the existence of fixed reality boxes IN OTHERS.

And indeed, as will gradually become apparent in the text ahead, recognizing fixed reality boxes in others is one of the most fundamental launch points for self-empowerment.

LEARNING TO RECOGNIZE REALITY BOXES

If it is considered that individuals have reality boxes, and that these might have something to do with influential limits of their awareness regarding self-empowerment, then two questions must emerge:

First, can individuals recognize their set limits of awareness?

Second, can they escape those limits, thereby increasing the scope of their awareness?

Well, one cannot usually perceive the limits of one's own reality boxes. But there is one way to activate cognitive realization of the nature of reality boxes -- to set about observing those not of self, but of others.

The implication here is that one might not be able to see one's own set reality box or boxes, because all one does is mentally pop around within them.

Observing the reality boxes of others, however, is an entirely different and much easier matter, one quite astonishing, amazing, and wondrous.

The foregoing is just one suggestive way of opening the concept that individuals are not JUST individuals. They are also walking, talking reality boxes -- each of which can best discriminate only in accord with how their reality boxes have become formatted and set.

One of the first steps toward empowerment therefore requires recognition of reality boxes per se, especially with respect to others, and, where possible, examining them for their constituents.

RECOMMENDED PASTIME ACTIVITY

ATTEMPT COVERTLY AND WITHOUT EMOTIONAL INVOLVEMENT TO STUDY THE REALITY BOXES OF OTHERS, ESPECIALLY WITH REGARD TO WHAT THEY DO AND DON'T INCLUDE AWARENESS of

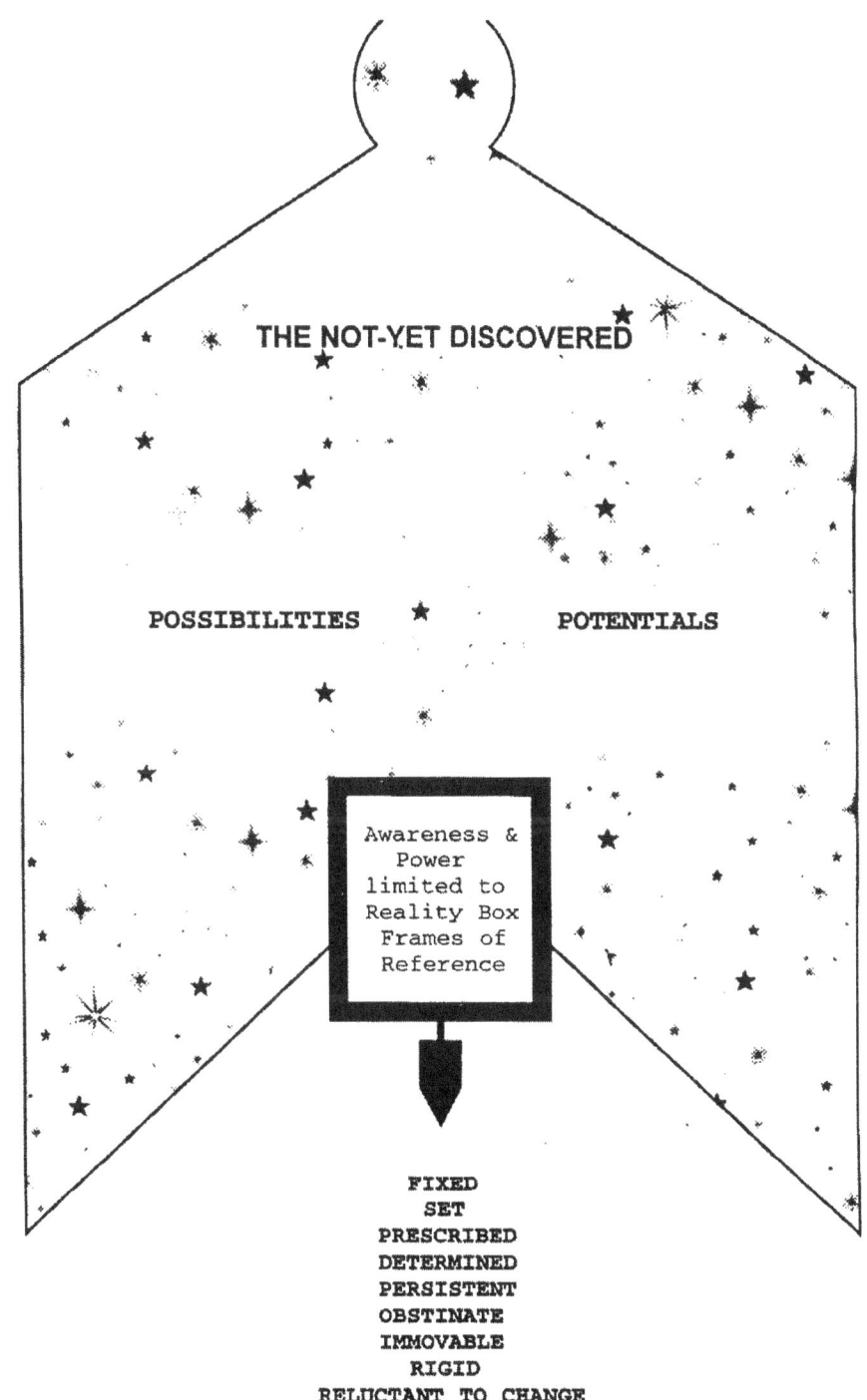

FIGURE 2.

Chapter 3

REALITY BOXES AND EMPOWERMENT MAPS

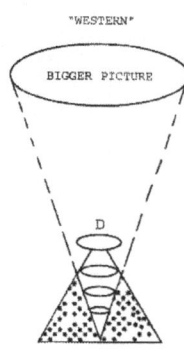

EVERYONE POSSESSES some kind of reality box, and that this IS so really needs to be accepted by anyone interested in power and empowerment.

As it is, people in general accept the idea of reality boxes, but perhaps under some other frame of reference -- for example, how one's head is wired, what one's mindset consists of, or whether one is playing with a full deck or not.

If groups of individuals possess similar reality boxes, then there is not much interest in them. But various kinds of interest, from marginal to highly dramatic, might arise when different reality boxes are encountered, especially if they are strategically different or downright incompatible.

Most interest in reality boxes usually focuses on what is in them, if such can be perceived and brought to light. This kind of interest is fair enough, especially with regard to mundane and average affairs.

But there are certain areas of life in which what is MISSING or ABSENT in reality boxes is far more important than what is in them.

One of these areas involves power and empowerment. If for no other reason, this can easily be deduced from the fact that keeping others unknowledgeable and ignorant of empowerment faculties and methods is a full part of so-called power games.

Those whose reality boxes contain little or no knowledge of empowerment faculties and methods constitute easy herds for power manipulators and managers.

This kind of thing (discussed at length in Volume I) equates to the so-called status quo among most societal power structures that have dominion, influence, and control over the bodies, minds, and economic and educational assets and potentials of the many.

Thus, the principal problem with respect to empowerment is not what is in reality boxes, but what is missing from them in terms of information and knowledge.

In this sense, the principal goal is to add information and knowledge into reality boxes, rather than to attempt to reorganize, correct, or re-edit what is already therein.

There are two factors about reality boxes that are seldom touched upon, largely because the boxes are usually experienced and perceived as fixed in nature.

First, reality boxes are usually identified by the information they contain, which is translated into behavior and attitudes that can be recognized, and which can be judged, accepted, or rejected by the reality boxes of others.

Second, and in more basic fact, reality boxes are merely mental configurations, or configurations of mind.

These configurations can indeed exist in long-term, fixed states or conditions. But the configurations can, and will, reconfigure if and when new information is encountered -- providing the information is SENSED and FELT as viable, pro-survival, and additive to the energizing of empowerment and self-power.

How this will take place at the individual level is difficult to say or establish. Based on in-depth historical evidence, one thing is for sure: MIND will probably not reconfigure its reality boxes all that much, simply as the result of mere intellectual exercise -- because, on average, intellectual data alone does not predict eventual outcomes,

This may be difficult to grok at first. However, sense can be made if we think of reality boxes not only as a collection of information and knowledge, but as a mind MAP, or, even better, as a deep-mind map.

Indeed, mind does not deal too well with random or confused bits of information or knowledge, unless it is possible to arrange, organize, and juxtapose the bits into a bigger picture or a more encompassing scenario.

In any event, that mind organizes information, for better or worse, can hardly be argued.

And it is understood quite well that if mind is presented with information already organized or mapped, then the process of assimilation is easier because mind can more easily sense and recognize not only the whole of it, but its implications also.

As discussed in Volume I, the easiest and best way to ensure depowerment is to prevent effective information about empowerment and power from being adequately organized and mapped. It is quite certain that ensuring and perpetuating depowerment of the many is in fact one of the basic strategies of societal dominion of power by the few.

Based on the foregoing considerations, empowerment (or, perhaps, re-empowerment) at the individual level requires not only information about empowerment, but also various kinds of maps that organize the otherwise random information into a bigger whole.

As will become more evident in the chapters ahead, the power to make maps of anything and everything is clearly an innate human power. Indeed, maps activate the innate powers having to do with making bigger-picture sense of anything.

TWO MAJOR METHODS OF ORGANIZING KNOWLEDGE

It is now useful to point out that there are two historical and major methods that can be used to examine and study phenomena, information, and knowledge. These have traditionally been referred to as the Western and the Eastern methods.

The WESTERN method starts with smaller pictures, isolating their bits and pieces and parts, and then attempting to erect a bigger picture or a larger totality.

This concept is often referred to as the bottom-upward method and is especially characteristic of the modern European material sciences in the cultural West.

The EASTERN method starts with a bigger picture, and then attempts to discover the bits and pieces and parts that fit within it.

This concept is sometimes referred to as the top-downward method and was characteristic of Asian studies regarding what life consists of.

Both methods have their strong and weak points, and in the past various debates have gone on as to which is more productive.

What is usually ignored, however, is that both methods descend from the versatile human mind, and which shows that the generic mind of our species can think from the bottom up as well as from the top down. So there is no real point in getting stuck in one method or the other -- and certainly not if one is interested in empowerment.

However, it is important to point up that "the individual" as such is a small bit, piece, or part within the bigger picture of the human species overall.

Innate powers cannot exist within the individual unless they first exist within the species. This is almost the same as saying that innate powers download from the species level into the level of individuals, whether multiple or singular.

So, although individuals like to think in personal terms about THEIR powers and THEIR empowerment, when and if empowerment begins to unfold within them it will do so within the bigger-picture power contexts around them.

INDIVIDUAL EMPOWERMENT AS INCREASE OF POWER CAPACITY AND DYNAMISM

The idea of individual empowerment carries the nuance of increase of power capacity and dynamism. And so, as with the Western method, the examination of diverse bits and pieces that might contribute to the increase is justified.

But in the end, all diverse bits and pieces are parts of a bigger map or a larger system, and information about these is as important as is any individual idea of what empowerment consists of.

The bigger maps or systems are made up of bits and pieces, of course. But without the map one may not know where and how to fit together the bits and pieces into the larger capacity and dynamism. If an encyclopedia of human powers did exist, it would constitute a map of them.

In one sense, then, this volume needs to be map-like. In a companion sense, it is also a beginning encyclopedia of human powers -- to which others now and in future need to contribute.

AS AN EASY INTELLECTUAL EXERCISE

TAKE SOME TIME TO CONSULT A DICTIONARY REGARDING THE DEFINITIONS OF "MAP" AND "ENCYCLOPEDIA" THEN FIGURE OUT WHAT PURPOSES THE DEFINITIONS MIGHT SERVE WITH REGARD TO EMPOWERMENT

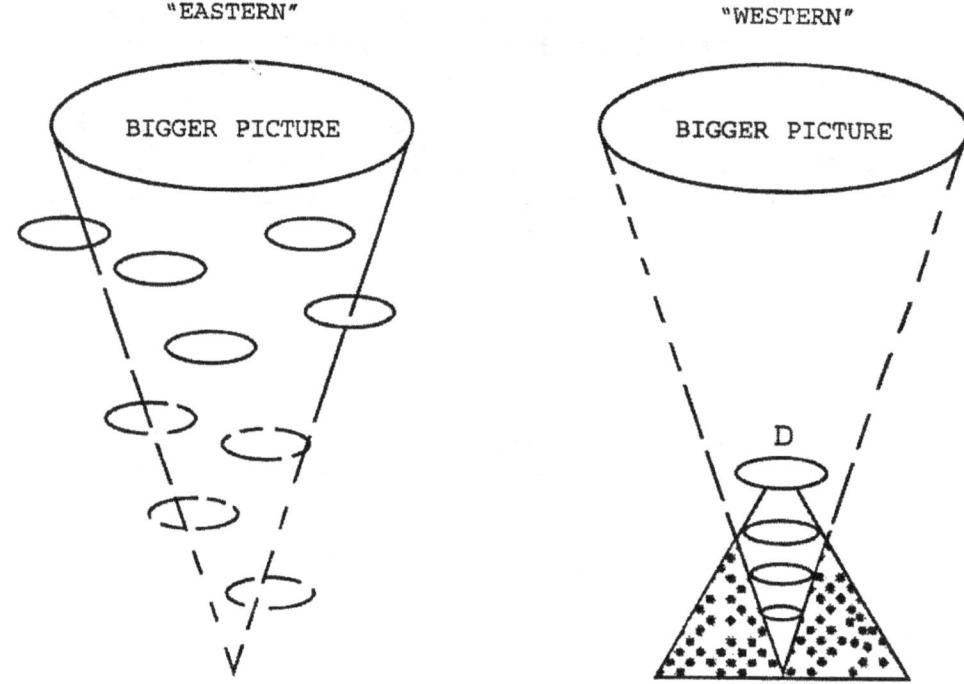

KEY:

⬭ - smaller picture reality.

D = Dominant smaller picture reality.

FIGURE 3. The configurations of the Eastern and Western methods for examining phenomena can be quite blurred, and some modern approaches combine elements of both. Both methods have deficits. But the Western method, sometimes referred to as "reductionism," can be very limiting in that a smaller, reductionistic reality is likely to achieve dominance, thereby excluding evidence and realities that do not fit with it. For example, the idea that some are born gifted with powers while others are not is reductionistic. This is a smaller picture pseudo-reality that can be groked as such if the bigger picture of our species powers is identified and considered. Bigger pictures usually contain numerous smaller ones. The Eastern method favors easy recognition of this, while the Western method does not. Collection of evidence is more easily assimilated via the Eastern method, while the collection of evidence via the Western method can remain fractured and unassimilated.

Chapter 4

THREE MAJOR CATEGORIES OF EMPOWERMENT AND POWER

OBSERVATION OVER time and in-depth will gradually reveal that there are at least three major categories of information about power and empowerment.

Each of these categories can be seen as substantive bigger pictures composed of numerous parts, and each one of the three is as important as the other two.

However, there are enormous differences regarding their visibility. The most visible category has to do with social and societal activities and their resulting power structures.

Social and societal power activities collect around the highly hypnoid-like idea that power consists of control, influence, and authority by the few over the many others who then exist in this or that state of physical and mental subservience.

This idea is exceedingly powerful and influential, and, it may as well be added, serious in nature and in implementation.

There are many idealizing and utopian concepts about empowerment that seek to diminish and to ignore the importance of societal power phenomena and activities.

But in the end, and as history demonstrates, not having informed knowledge about how societal power structures are set up and maintained can have far-reaching consequences.

In any event, empowerment consists of expanding, not contracting, one's overall knowledge, especially with respect to any and all power phenomena. So societal power phenomena should be dissected as deeply as possible -- as was attempted in Volume I of this series.

Although this category is visible, in-depth dissection reveals that only about 20 percent of it is visible, while the remaining greater percentage is, by design, hidden from the subservient populations.

Once THIS is brought to light, the reason why so much is hidden is quite understandable. If the few are to have societal power over the many, then the many must somehow be kept in some kind of depowered condition.

Thus, the ways and means of empowerment need to be made unavailable. It is this that accounts for the almost total absence of socially supported power schools, of encyclopedias itemizing all factors having to do with power, empowerment, and descriptions of innate human powers.

One of the results of this particular absence is that most do not really know what their powers are.

And so the full spectrum of human powers remains invisible -- but only because it has not been brought into visibility and communal realization.

WHAT human powers consist of, especially at the species and at the individual levels, altogether constitutes one of the three major categories that can be identified as such.

It is now the task of this Volume II to contribute to increasing the visibility of innate human powers, and which constitute the second major category of information about power and empowerment.

Beyond the two categories just mentioned, there exists a major category that deserves several descriptions from different points of view, and which, overall, is most invisible.

But generally speaking here, it consists of sympathetic and harmonic activity between and among, as it were, more fully awakened minds of individuals.

There may be other important and major categories of power and empowerment. But the categories of societal powers, individual powers, and harmonic powers among individuals do exist.

Please note that this writer has resisted the temptation to enumerate these categories as 1, 2, and 3. Doing so would give the impression of priority, when in observable fact each of the categories has equal importance and meaning.

One might not easily perceive this equality at first, usually because the concepts of human interconnectedness have first to be opened up for discussion.

SUGGESTED STUDY

STRETCH THE LIMITS OF ONE'S REALITY BOX AND MAKE A LIST OF AS MANY TYPES OF POWER AS POSSIBLE

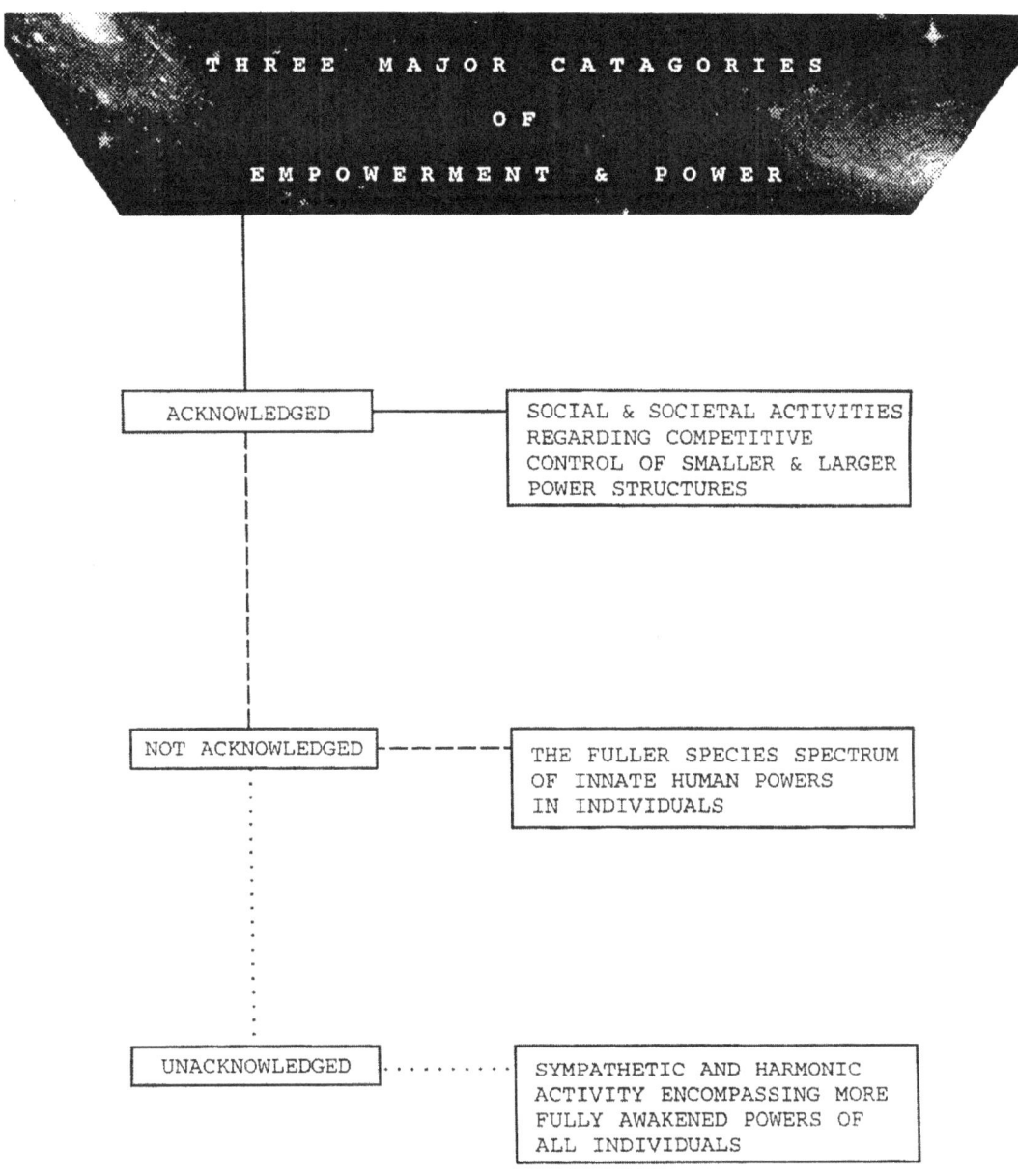

FIGURE 4.

Chapter 5

THE VITALIZATION OF EMPOWERMENT

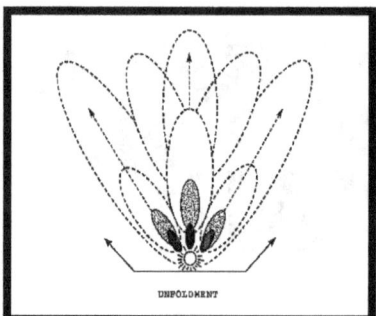

THERE ARE many factors that contribute to the overall emergence and unfoldment of empowerment.

Two initial problems arise because of this multiplicity.

First, anything that is made up of multiple factors cannot be understood or grasped in one swoop of intellectual excitement, especially if the factors exist outside of one's reality box.

After all, one cannot incorporate what one has never heard of before.

To get anywhere with the multiplicity, its factors must patiently be separated and identified one-by-one so that they can be added into one's reality box and thereby become working power factors within one's overall mind.

Second, the multiplicity makes it difficult to know where to start the one-by-one identification process.

With respect to this, there is a natural tendency for individuals to assume they can begin empowerment in the light of whatever is already within their reality boxes.

This may be workable in some cases. But on average, those who feel relatively powerless don't have much of the wherewithal for empowerment included and activated in their reality boxes.

In any event, power is always a relationship between what is inside and outside of any given individual reality box. And so, one must look outside of self in order to identify factors that, so to speak, can call forth empowerment from within.

AN ESSENTIAL ASPECT OF POWER

With the two basic problems of the multiplicity now pointed out, it might be seen that the essential nature of power provides a very good clue as to where one might start.

However power might be thought of, it clearly consists of various kinds of vital energy and force.

Indeed, anything that is energy-less and force-less can hardly be considered as power -- and this equally applies to whatever is inside and outside of reality boxes. Thus, any such lessness can logically be identified as conditions of depowerment.

VITAL - VITALITY – VITALIZATION

To proceed beyond this starting point, it is necessary to consider the definitions of the term VITAL.

In its modern sense, the word is defined as "existing as a manifestation of life, and concerned with or necessary to the maintenance of life, and life organs."

However, the term entered English many centuries ago, at about 1386. At that time, it referred to "that immaterial force or principle which is present in living beings or organisms and by which they are animated, and their functions maintained."

By about 1593, the term also referred to "faculties, functions, powers, etc., inherent in or exhibited by living things or organic bodies."

During the twentieth century, the importance of these older definitions was diminished, largely because the modern sciences were unable (and are still unable) to explain how animate life becomes animated.

There are certainly difficulties regarding how animated life is to be understood as coming into existence.

But there is no problem at all in comprehending the concept of to DE-VITALIZE -- i.e., "to deprive of life or vitality," and which, of course, is certainly the direct equivalent of DE-POWERMENT.

One of the implications of this is that at least a minimal working knowledge of depowerment is as important as knowledge of empowerment. This becomes rather clear if one considers the plus and minus energies involved between vitalized and devitalized powers.

SUGGESTED EXERCISE

TRY TO OBSERVE ANYTHING THAT EXHIBITS DEVITALIZED VITALITY AND/OR CONDITIONS

Chapter 6

RECOGNITION OF EMPOWERMENT PROCESSES

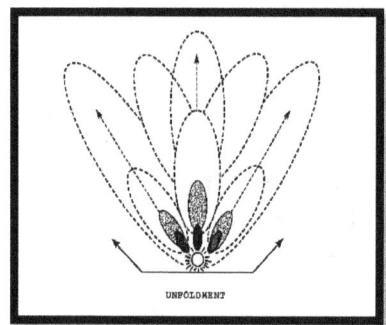

OPENING DOORS of perception into matters that have never been identified before might be difficult at first. And so the two factors discussed in this chapter might seem challenging at first, but only because one is not already familiar with them.

The first has to do with the fact that human powers have never been described as a spectrum that is somehow self-organized. So human powers have hardly ever been discussed in any organizing way, largely because doing so would contribute to more extensive knowledge about them.

The second factor is quite subtle. It consists of an attempt to show that human powers recognize empowerment information -- and do so whether one is aware of it or not, and even if one is consciously unaware of the existence of the powers.

While this might seem far out at first, it is generally understood that a lot of mind-dynamic activities do take place without our being consciously aware of them. And indeed, becoming consciously aware of those otherwise invisible activities constitutes one of the proverbial ladders of empowerment.

One of the principal problems involved here has to do with how to define "empowerment information."

This is at first difficult because the general idea of information is that it is something that one can elect to utilize or not.

It is rather obvious that at the conscious level one can elect to utilize whatever information one becomes conscious of. It is equally the case that human systems are always being bombarded with information beneath conscious perception of it.

The most common idea about information is that it does exist, that it is available, that it is discoverable, that it just sits around until the conscious intellectual part of a human mind encounters it and then decides to utilize it or not.

In other words, it is commonly thought that information, of and in itself, is inert -- i.e., has no power to move itself, is deficient in active properties, and remains at rest unless acted upon by some force external to it.

In keeping with this broadly shared idea about information, it can thus be thought that an information or knowledge package is inert, and stays at rest unless or until it is consciously discovered and acted upon.

However, as many past and present societal mind-conditioners and disinformation agents have long realized, information always IMPLIES something, and between the information and what it implies is always motion of some kind.

In other words, information is not inert. It is dynamic. Indeed, if information did not imply anything, then it would not be considered as information at all.

SURVIVAL vs REALITY BOXES

The limitations of reality boxes of course can curtail perception of implications, especially at the conscious or surface levels of awareness and socially conditioned intelligence.

If human organisms were, for their survival, totally and only dependent on the limits of their reality boxes, most of them would not get much beyond the get-go.

There certainly would not be much if any empowerment, largely because empowerment clearly implies a needed escape from the confines of reality boxes that work to disable it.

A question now emerges, one that seems never to have been asked before. Can human organisms recognize empowerment information in ways that transcend the limits *of* their reality boxes?

The surprising answer is Yes -- but the answer rests upon grounds that are so extremely subtle that few have recognized them, even when dwelling amid them.

Backing up for a moment, it is worthwhile wondering if the human species throughout its duration has failed to accumulate what might be called a reservoir of empowering information-plus-implications.

It can be demonstrated that no encyclopedias of power and empowerment have ever seen the light of day.

The absence of these is determined by the machinations of societal power-control affairs manufactured within the species -- the same species that also manifests wisdom and wisdom-like information.

It is quite possible to think that wisdom, or anything akin to it, is more empowering than, say, non-wisdom, ignorance, or depowerment, and which are also manufactured within power-control social systems.

And so yet another question emerges. Where and how has wisdom-like, hence empowering, information escaped the depowerment mechanisms of social power-control structures?

THE NATURE OF APHORISMS

An APHORISM is defined as "a concise statement of a principle, a terse formulation of a truth or sentiment."

But the functional nature of aphorisms is to encapsulate specific information-plus-implication packages that are so apparent that they can transcend the limits of all kinds of reality boxes.

The implications contained in aphorisms also transcend time and historical epochs and tend to be relevant and applicable wherever individuals of our species gather and incorporate together in any way.

Indeed, if aphorisms do not cross time and transcend lesser particulars of our socio-intelligent species, then they are useless in the same way that inert information is.

WHAT BECOMES UNDERSTOOD BECOMES USEFUL

Included in the concise aphorisms presented at the front of this book is one by the American essayist, John Jay Chapman (1862-1933), pointing up that "There are plenty of people to whom the crucial problems of their lives never get presented in terms they can understand."

It is quite clear that matters of human powers and empowerment are usually "crucial problems."

But it is equally clear that such problems are so convulsed within social and societal machinations that they are hardly ever presented in terms, concise or otherwise, that people can understand.

It is something of a habit, installed culturally, that people think they need to discover NEW stuff in order to increase understanding.

There is, of course, great merit in such discovering, so much so that one can fall into the trap of thinking that imbibing the new is the only way to increase understanding. When the new is integrated into what one already knows, then increase of understanding can take place.

This concept is certainly functional IF the new is really new -- which is to say, having never before appeared within the contexts of human knowledge packages.

However, the crucial problems of power and empowerment are NOT new.

They are, in fact, rather old, and (as almost anyone can realize) are cluttered with confusions of smoke and mirrors that are deliberately installed on behalf of societal power structure controls.

Even so, the crucial problems of power and empowerment ARE problems of discovery, not of the new, but of the socio-human dynamics of something that is very old-power and control of it.

One of the great literary figures of the modern age, the French novelist Marcel Proust (1871-1922), produced a. concise aphorism that is relevant to discovery in general: "The real voyage of discovery consists not in seeking new landscapes, but in having new eyes."

With this, Proust merely echoed a discovered wisdom package of many others before him, that whether the new or the old is involved, the "eyes" will in the end determine what is seen or not.

In this context, "eyes" is one of the chief metaphors for reality boxes.

It is also fair to extend the metaphor so as to indicate that one can exist amid something (such as the panorama of human powers) but have "eyes" that see less than half of it, or perhaps little or none of it at all.

The "eyes" metaphor can also be extended to include all human sensing systems, active or inactive.

The foregoing discussion has had a functional purpose with respect to the critical problems of human powers.

That purpose is to open up consideration of what "eyes" see, both literally and figuratively, in the contexts of the critical problems of human powers, and especially what they see the best and easiest.

In this sense, it is interesting to wonder why aphorisms come into existence, transcend socio-political and cultural barriers as they do, and are perpetuated through centuries and time.

APHORISMS and RELEVANCE

As mentioned earlier, average dictionaries will indicate that an aphorism is "a terse and concise formulation of a truth or sentiment." This, however, is a rather weak description for something that gets perpetuated through centuries of fluctuating history and across cultural barriers.

A more intimate examination of the nature of aphorisms (and of maxims and adages as well) can reveal that they are concise formulations not so much of truth or sentiment, but as references to factors that are RELEVANT to the on-going human condition through time and centuries.

Furthermore, the relevancy is recognizable through time by some aspect of human consciousness that is independent of educational, cultural, or social class machinations -- and which aphorisms indeed transcend.

This is the same as saying that aphorisms, in general, transcend reality boxes that become formatted because of educational, cultural, or social class machinations, and which can be radically different.

If over decades and centuries the recognizable relevancy of aphorisms transcend time and reality boxes, then it becomes something of a seminal question as to what, exactly, it is in human consciousness that perceives the relevancy.

The time transcending factor indicates that whatever it is that perceives, the relevancy is not acquired within the contexts of reality boxes isolated in their contemporary times.

Rather, the perceiving of the relevancy must be affected by some kind of innate, rather than acquired, functions that operate outside of the limits or boundaries of reality boxes.

Indeed, the continuing and on-going relevancy of aphorisms cannot be recognized unless there is something that does the recognizing.

These considerations bring up another factor having to do with why the relevancy of aphorisms should be recognized in the first place.

After all, aphorisms are made up out of a mere few words, which might mean nothing -- unless the idea they altogether express resonates with something in overall human consciousness and does so independently of whatever reality box limits are present.

The modern definitions given to the term RELEVANT refer to "bearing upon the matter at hand; pertinent; implying a traceable, significant, logical connection."

But the term RELEVANT is taken from the Latin RELEVARE, defined as "to raise up," while in English the term RAISE is essentially defined as "to awaken, arouse, or incite."

And here it now becomes recognizable that to awaken, arouse, activate, incite, or excite equate to some of the definitions of EMPOWERMENT.

Chapter 7

THE SPECTRUM OF HUMAN POWERS

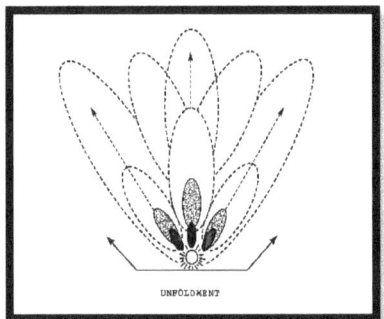

HUMAN POWERS obviously belong to the human organism. However, it is not understood very well what that organism actually consists of in any sense that can be thought of as complete.

There are many influential ideas about this matter, but they hold water only if numerous aspects of the human organism are ignored or not incorporated.

It is fair to state this because it is frequently mentioned, in the sciences and elsewhere, that there are many "mysteries" about the human organism that elude explanation.

One of those mysteries pertains to the human powers, with questions still outstanding about why and how they exist, and where they can be incorporated into an overall structural schematic.

As mentioned in chapter 3, the substantive existence of human powers is not portrayed in maps of the mind, and certainly not with any emphasis on their importance.

NO MAPS OF HUMAN POWERS

It is thus that there are no maps of human powers that are clearly identified as such. And so it is difficult to consider how they consist together in the scope of something that might be referred to as an inclusive power package.

It is because of this that although human powers can be discussed in words, they cannot be pictured in overall ways that equate to something akin to an anatomical chart.

If one spends a great deal of time trying to study what the human consists of, one can discover that about the only factor altogether agreed on is that the human is an organism. Indeed, all life forms are completely accepted as organisms, and any debates that follow thereafter refer only to their internal details. However, the debates about the details can become so introverting that the important concept of the human as an organism can become minimalized or fall to the wayside altogether.

With respect to human powers, and to many other human factors as well, the concept of the human as an organism needs to be restored to its essential importance, and by doing so it becomes possible to conceptualize them as an inclusive power package.

DEFINITIONS OF ORGANISM

In most languages, the term ORGANISM is understood to have two important definitions:

1. A complete structure of interdependent and subordinate elements whose relations and properties are largely determined by their function in the whole;
2. An individual constituted to carry on the activities of life by means of organs separate in function but mutually dependent.

It seems to be generally thought that the definitions of the term derive from the words ORGANIC and ORGAN, and which is the case in part.

But the definitions are more derived from the terms ORGANIZE which is generally defined as:

- To arrange or form into a coherent unity or functioning whole;
- To integrate;
- To arrange elements by systematic planning and united effort so as to result in a whole of interdependent parts.

The link between ORGANIC and ORGANIZE is that all life forms demonstrate internal organizations of parts that constitute their interdependent whole -- and WITHOUT WHICH those life forms could not survive or even exist.

Thus, although it can be thought that an organism is a life-form package, it is, by necessity, an organized package -- and if it were not organized, then Zippo and down the tubes it goes.

This is somewhat like saying that although a life form can exist, or learn to exist, amid chaos, it will NOT exist (for very long) if its internal organization becomes unorganized to any relevant degree.

With regard to human organisms, it is clear that they possess innate powers, if only in potential, inactive, or not consciously realized states. It is quite possible to assume that if human organisms did NOT have innate powers, then they could not exist as the life forms they are.

If it is accepted that human organisms possess innate powers, then it must follow that matters relevant to their organization AND disorganization are important and significant.

And it must therefore follow that ANY realizing sense of organization of powers must be better than no sense of it at all.

There must be many ways to conceptualize, discuss, and diagram, how human powers are organized -- and which conceptualizing simply refers to what powers do exist, consciously enumerating them, and then realizing how they are interconnected (or "wired") throughout the human organism entire. There are only two real problems involved here:

A. Trenchant social conditioning against doing anything of the kind, and all that implies;
B. And the fact, ultimately to be discovered, of HOW MANY powers (known or unknown) that individual human organisms actually possess, and all THAT implies.

At the all-inclusive species level, and thus with respect to all its produced individuals, humans cannot have just a few discrete, non-interacting powers, for if they did then all human things would be more simple and straightforward than they obviously are.

It is thus that one can assume to have a large number of powers (known or unknown), and if one undertakes to make lists of them, it soon becomes apparent that at least many of the powers interact with each other.

But this is exactly in keeping with the fundamental concept of interdependent organization via which the whole of an organism is interactive.

One useful way to conceptualize the whole of human powers is via the definition of a SPECTRUM:

"A continuous sequence or range; an array of components separated and arranged in the order of some varying characteristic."

The use of the spectrum metaphor facilitates a bigger picture thinking about human powers as constituting both separate powers, but which, when needed, can blend together in some kind of continuous range or sequence of empowerment.

However, there are many other useful ways to conceptualize powers -- the sole criteria being that one must undertake the conceptualizing in any form possible and informative.

PART TWO
UNIDENTIFIED PARTS OF MIND

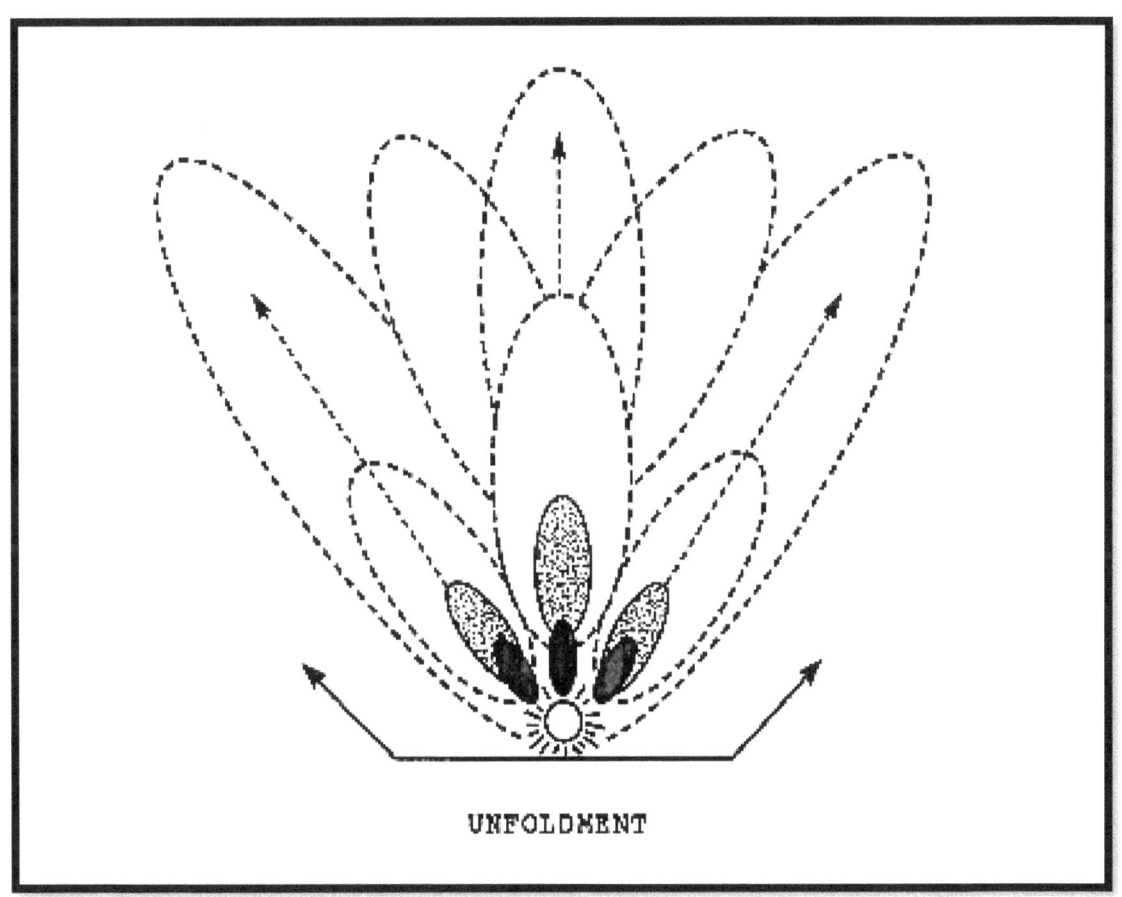

UNFOLDMENT

Chapter 8

MAPS OF THE MIND

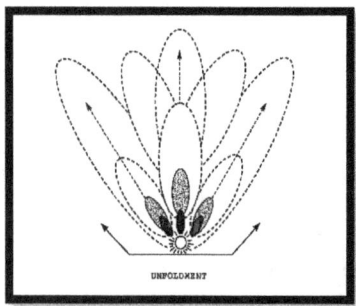

IT IS commonly understood that mind has "parts." This is to say that the mind is composed of various activities and functions, some of which can be recognized as different enough so as to take on part-like distinctions.

Dividing the mind into various parts has a long and often complicated history stretching back into antiquity. Tracing this history from various sources makes for fascinating reading and can be informative, and those interested in empowerment might thereby add important elements to their reality boxes.

One convenient source for such maps is Charles Hampden-Turner's 1981 book entitled MAPS OF THE MIND: CHARTS AND CONCEPTS OF THE MIND AND ITS LABYRINTHS -- some sixty maps are neatly drawn together in this very elegant book.

This book is quite wonderful, to be sure, and well worth taking time to study its contents. However, human powers, innate or otherwise, are not mentioned with respect to any of the sixty maps portrayed in the book.

And, in the end, one can be left wondering why the mind should have sixty maps, each quite different.

Perhaps one lesson that can be drawn in this respect is that the mind and its parts can be formatted in different ways, while the formats themselves can undergo constant recombination.

This is to suggest that whatever the mind might consist of, it is a recombinant "vehicle" that can be formatted, reformatted, and recombined in accord with perceived needs.

Most people, on average, might have but little awareness of maps, or models, of the mind, especially so many as sixty of them.

But it is obvious that empowerment, the mind, and reality boxes are all somehow interrelated, and that all of them somehow function, so to speak, with respect to information they do or do not have.

It can be thought that INFORMATION is of extreme importance to a species having extensive intelligence, and if this were not so, then it is difficult to discern the purpose of having intelligence in the first place.

Even if this is hard to grok, it is clear that functions of mind can be shaped not just by experience, but also by information that is available or not available.

And one merely has to consider the issues that surround social programming efforts that are always busy managing information this way and that.

It is also possible to consider that one's plus or minus power status is more or less commensurate with information that does or does not exist in one's reality boxes. Thus, ANY information about empowerment that can be added into reality boxes is better than adding no such information at all.

The intelligent mind, and all that is relative to it, constitutes perhaps the most extremely complicated factor in human life overall.

It is complicated because of confusions that arise to surround it -- especially those confusions that are not identified AS confusions, and are thus double confusions, of all things.

Many of these double confusions work to derail concepts of empowerment.

At least some of the confusions have one factor in common: they exist because certain parts of mind have not been identified or accepted as such.

Indeed, parts of mind that have something to do with power and empowerment at the individual level are almost certainly to be shrouded in confusions because of any number of social control reasons described at length elsewhere in this series.

Chapter 9

THE ON-GOING CONFUSION OF POWERS-MIND-INTELLIGENCE

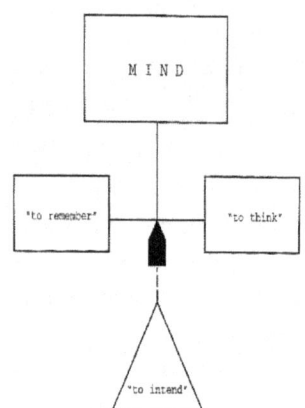

IT IS possible to think that human powers, human mind, and human intelligence have something to do with each other.

With respect to this, however, it should be pointed out that orthodox knowledge packages about the mind that have evolved during the modern period do not include concepts that bring these three factors together.

The principal reason for this is that all issues about human powers are avoided because of socio-cultural programming designed to achieve the avoidance. Thus, the mind is studied and examined without including this important aspect of human existence.

Any approach to empowerment, however, must include some kind of discussion along these lines, if only because a bigger picture of empowerment must eventually include knowledge packages about mind-dynamic functions that lead to empowerment.

THE ACKNOWLEDGEMENT OF HUMAN POWERS IN PRE-MODERN TIMES

If one studies the history of concepts of the mind, it will certainly be discovered that our pre-modern predecessors did not think of it via the all-encompassing thing-in-itself concept that became so socially prevalent only during the last third of the nineteenth century.

Furthermore, a study of how powers were viewed in the pre-modern past shows that although the existence of mind was considered important enough, individuals were seldom judged by their minds. They were judged by the powers they were manifesting or not manifesting.

In this sense, it seems that minds took second place with respect to powers being manifested, and that it was in fact powers manifesting that were of major concern for any number of important reasons.

If this is meditated upon as calmly as possible, it is possible to discern that although all individuals can be thought of as having a mind, there are actually great distinctions between those manifesting powers and those not doing so.

DISTINCTIONS BETWEEN MIND AND POWERS

One such distinction has to do with the rather visible reality that those manifesting powers are something to be dealt with and taken seriously.

And against this distinction, whether or not all have minds is clearly of lesser significance.

And something like this is STILL in process of happening just about everywhere. Although the issues of human powers have been deeply submerged beneath otherwise scientific, philosophic, and psychological concepts of mind, individuals are STILL not recognized and judged by the minds they have, but by their overall power status.

One identifiable reason for this is the common knowledge that one can have a so-called brilliant mind, but have no power. In fact, a brilliant mind sans power is just a "nerd," or something similar in different lingoes.

It is also generally understood, at least somewhat, that those demonstrating this or that kind of power might not have too much MIND going for them. Even so, such will attract great attention.

For more clarity here, a society based upon powers manifesting in this or that individual is clearly a society different from one based on the idea that everyone has a mind.

The principal reason is that minds NOT extending and actualizing their powers can be thought of as powerless, and as such do not need to be as seriously considered as those who do manifest them.

As pre-modern times developed into what we recognize as modern times, it gradually became possible to study and research the human mind without incorporating research into the nature of human powers -- and especially not incorporating any empowerment research that might focus on activating powers within individuals.

As has been discussed throughout Volume I, and AGAIN to emphasize, it is not generally realized that power-cum-empowerment knowledge is almost totally absent, not only within societal structures in general, but also within the contexts of the modern studies of mind.

A very large archive of mind research came into existence, especially during the twentieth century, and since that archive IS large and extensive, it also seems authoritative. So it is possible to think of it as more important than almost anything else.

But this archive is almost totally deficit with respect to knowledge about human powers. It is thus possible to immerse oneself into studies of the mind without ever encountering the topic of empowerment of human powers,

The basic reason for going into all this is that most individuals will automatically assume that powers and minds are not only somehow relative to each other. One might even assume that concepts of mind are more important than the actual existence of human powers.

In any event, assuming a connection between mind and powers is one thing. Trying to find out what the mind IS, is another matter -- one vastly complicated by, believe it or not, the vast number of definitions and models of MIND.

A THREE-PART MODEL OF MIND CIRCA 1250 A.D.

If one consults the Oxford Dictionary of the English language, it will be revealed that definitions for MIND, together with permutations, number over seventy.

What this large multiplicity of definitions signifies is not at all clear, except that mind must be a very complicated thing.

The term MIND (MYND) entered English (and other European languages) at about the year 1000. While its derivation is not certain, that it principally referred to "memory" is quite clear. In its original sense, it might have also had, and soon came to have, combined nuances of "to think, to remember, to intend."

The term INTEND is taken, via Old French, from the Latin INTENDERE, basically meaning "to stretch out or forth, extend, strain, expand, increase, intensify, purpose, endeavor, assert."

As this bit of nomenclature research establishes, what came to be called the MIND was early divided up into three principal parts: the "to think" part, the "to remember" part, and the "to intend" part.

It is quite probable that people at the beginning of the second millennium were not too stupid, and that they would recognize that the "to think" and "to remember" parts were passive and harmless enough, but that the "to intend" part was entirely a different matter.

That part was, and still is, entirely redolent of both potential and actualizing power(s). And if understood that way, the issues involved soon become a matter of profound concern.

That concern can easily be traced backward into antiquity -- as well as forward into present times, and into the future as well -- within the familiar perspective of who is to have and not have power.

If one traces the nomenclature developments relevant to this three-part concept of mind, then it is possible to discover that although the passive parts "to think" and "to remember" are interesting enough, the active "to intend" part demands special treatment -- mainly involving how to control and contain it.

And the best way to achieve such control and containment, in the eyes of societal power managers at least, is to not permit any knowledge packages to accumulate about that part -- for the intended part clearly has too much to do with power and empowerment.

Thereafter, definitions of the mind can otherwise become very numerous on behalf of examining the nature of the two passive parts, and this multiplicity of definitions was naturally extended into the proliferations of twentieth century psychologies.

NUMEROUS MODERN DEFINITIONS OF MIND

The very numerous modern definitions of mind have caused many to observe that although psychology has traditionally been defined as the science that deals with mental activities, no commonly agreed-upon definition of mind has yet come forth.

Indeed, during the twentieth century, various polls of numerous psychologists turned up an equal number of definitions.

Even so and overall, as of 1967, one definition for mind seems broadly to have been accepted as the most important one -- that MIND is "the organized totality of psychological processes which enables the individual to adapt to and interact with his environment."

The last few words of this definition, however, could be amended to read: ". . . to passively adapt and interact with his environment."

In any event, this definition continues to have great influence beyond 1967, and will probably continue to do so into the future.

There cannot be too much argument with this definition, largely because adapting to environments obviously reveals the existence of the human power to do so.

But it can be pointed out in order to challenge this limited definition, that mind exhibits other compelling phenomena in addition to merely adapting to whatever.

It can also be pointed out that adapting to environments includes adapting to whatever plus and minus circumstances are found in them.

Although it can be admitted that such adaptations do take place, they do not at all reflect the "organized totality of psychological processes" inherently and potentially available to each human individual.

For example, it is entirely possible to think that mind could adapt to the bigger scope of its own powers IF that scope was nurtured outside and independent of the lenses of given environments and circumstances, and which clearly demand passive conformity rather than intentional empowerment.

THE MOST FAVORED TWO-PART MODEL OF MIND
DURING THE TWENTIETH CENTURY

As will be elaborated ahead, many modernist ideas of mind abounded during the twentieth century.

Most of those ideas could be contained in or attributed to the two parts of mind that became fashionable and conventional during that century -- the conscious part, and the subconscious part.

Within the contexts of this two-part model, everything else about the mind could be considered as phenomena housed in, emanating from, or explained by one of those parts.

There was great cultural enthusiasm for this model, even though there remained a certain cloying difficulty that was simply overlooked or avoided. You see, neither of the two parts could themselves be EXPLAINED.

Even though the phrase "powers of mind" has been in use for several centuries, they are not attributed to either of the two parts. In discoverable fact, this topic is not only absent in conventional mind studies but is roughly derided if it is introduced -- especially with regard to "subliminal powers of mind."

The matter of human intelligence cannot be avoided altogether, in that having intelligence has for so long been extolled as one of the greatest hallmarks of our species.

Even so, and surprisingly, human intelligence is not attributed to either of the two parts. So intelligence is more or less in limbo, or might itself actually be an unidentified third part that is interactive with the other two parts.

In any event, in spite of its apparent two-part simplicity, this whole affair is so complicated that it might be passed over altogether (as many writers do).

But empowerment and mind and intelligence obviously have something to do with each other, and this relationship is, in some sense, a bigger picture of some kind.

THE CONCEPT OF "PARTS" OF THE MIND

Like definitions of mind, definitions of intelligence and powers are fraught with uncertainties and unknowns. But the definition of the term PART is quite definite and certain and is defined as:

> "An essential portion or integral element or one of the portions into which something is or is regarded as divided and which together constitute the whole."

The implication of this definition is that if a part is missing or is non-functioning, then the whole itself must begin altering toward non-functioning.

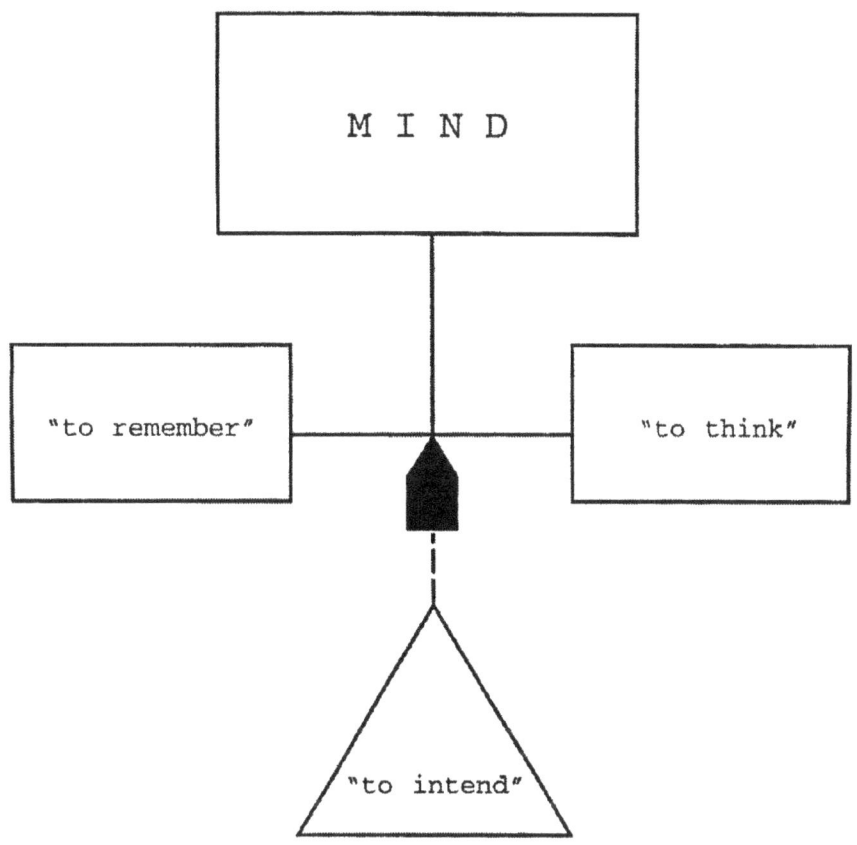

FIGURE 5. Rough diagram of the three-part concept of the Mind during the Late Middle Age circa the 13th to the 15th centuries. Activities ascribed to the "to intend" part were: to stretch out or fourth, extend, strain, expand, increase, intensify, purpose, endeavor, assert. Information regarding the "to intend" part was gradually obscured and made unavailable because of its direct relationship to power and power potentials, and which is still the case as this book is being written. Indeed, on many different levels, "to intend" is one of the major secrets of power involving actions and activities that must be kept undisclosed from any who might thwart them. Powers of intending are innate in our species, and in all individuals, for the functions of mind would clearly be seriously in jeopardy without them.

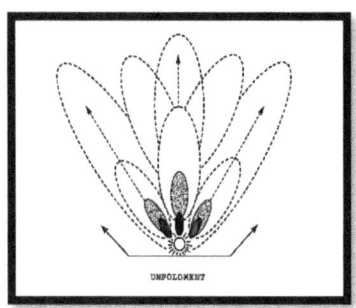

Chapter 10

THE PROBLEM OF KNOWING WHAT INTELLIGENCE IS

IF THERE is any interest in doing so, one can discover that some individuals think they cannot accumulate empowerment because their intelligence is insufficient or inadequate for that purpose.

It is quite possible that this notion reflects a reality box situation in which lurks some very limited kind of idea about intelligence that inhibits the unfolding of innate powers of mind and of empowerment.

Furthermore, this limited kind of idea about intelligence is broadly installed and shared via sociocultural conditioning processes -- largely because it seems to legitimize the familiar power structure distinctions between the more powerful, who are thought of as more intelligent, and the less powerful, who are assumed to be less intelligent.

In better reality, however, this is merely some kind of sociological propaganda -- in that examinations of power structures often reveal that the powerful may not really be all that intelligent, while many of the presumed powerless are more so.

THE CONTROL OF WHAT INTELLIGENCE IS THOUGHT TO BE

As already mentioned, one of the primary hallmarks of our species is that it possesses intelligence.

Another hallmark of our species, one less emphasized as such, is that it formats power structures that are more beneficial to the few and less than beneficial to the many.

In the sense of THIS hallmark, intelligence indwelling in individuals of the species cannot simply be allowed to manifest naturally, and certainly cannot be encouraged to do so far and wide.

Therefore, in the bigger pictures of societal power structures, it is at least necessary to keep real knowledge about intelligence as confused as possible. And, indeed, a historical survey of how intelligence has been thought of reflects the on-going existence of such confusions.

And even when searches regarding the nature of intelligence have taken place (as during the twentieth century), such searches have been characterized overall by-chains of theories, speculations, and experiments that have their day, but which, sooner or later, are replaced by new ideas and concepts.

The end result of this history so far is that what the essence or nature of intelligence IS has not yet been determined, and those attempting to do so are still at odds and embattled among themselves.

What has happened, however, is that certain ideas about the nature of intelligence have caught on, especially during recent modernist times. Those ideas have not only been accepted into general educational and academic processes, but various kinds of influential social programs have been built upon them.

It now transpires (as this book is being put together) that the authenticity of the influential modernist concepts is being challenged. And so the modernist ideas of what intelligence IS are themselves undergoing stress, crisis, and confusion.

Details of this stress and crisis can be found in several current sources; among which is a book entitled THE MAKING OF INTELLIGENCE (1999), by Ken Richardson.

Richardson's book is very interesting and easy enough to read, and also reveals a great deal about how intelligence has been considered.

A succinct blurb on the book's jacket indicates that "Concepts of intelligence wield a powerful influence on research into the brain and on how individuals progress in society. Yet, remarkably, there is still no agreed, scientific consensus about what this ubiquitous and adaptable concept means."

THE NATURE OF INTELLIGENCE AND THE NATURE OF EMPOWERMENT

One of the first difficulties in grasping the nature of intelligence hinges on the fact that it has traditionally been mis-identified as a "capacity" rather than as an innate power, or even as a part of the mind.

As indicated in chapter 8, a PART is defined as ONE of the ESSENTIAL portions or integral elements via which something is divided, and which together constitute the whole.

If, therefore, intelligence is subtracted as a PART of the human mind, it is then to be wondered what the mind would be like without it.

Furthermore, intelligence is obviously somehow linked to another part of the mind -- that "to intend" part, the nature of which has also been rendered into perpetual fogs of confusions.

If the intelligence part is subtracted from the "to intend" part, then it is decidedly to be wondered what the "to intend" part would be like.

But intelligence is not identified as a part of the mind, but rather as "a capacity," and sometimes as "a faculty."

A FACULTY is first defined as "ability, power, a natural aptitude, an abundance," and as "one of the powers of mind formerly held by psychologists to form the basis of all mental phenomena."

A CAPACITY is defined as "the ability to hold, receive, store, or accommodate." Implicit in the concept of capacity are the two subsidiary concepts of "maximum capacity" and "minimum capacity."

It is certainly clear enough that faculty and capacity are ASPECTS of intelligence, but only if intelligence is defined as an innate power. Otherwise, it would be difficult to see what faculty and capacity are aspects of.

As earlier discussed, a human power is best defined as an innate, inborn source or means of supplying energy -- and which is capable of magnification, of decrease, of being latent and untapped, or of being deenergized or depowered.

Indeed, the synonyms for POWER are usually given as force, energy, strength, might -- all of which can be latent or exerted physically and/or mentally.

While it is cumbersome to recount or synopsize the history of ideas about intelligence, it is relatively easy to discover and examine the successive definitions attributed to it.

INTELLIGENCE AND UNDERSTANDING

Even though the term INTELLIGENCE was not broadly used in English (or in French) until the sixteenth century, it appears to have entered into English at about 1390, and was taken from the Latin INTELEGENTIA which meant "understanding."

The first English definition is therefore given as "the faculty of understanding."

By about 1430, however, the definition was amended so as to read; "Understanding as a quality admitting of degree; specifically, as superior understanding; quickness of mental apprehension and sagacity."

At about 1450, the definition was extended as; "The action or fact of mentally apprehending something; understanding, knowledge, cognizance, comprehension (OF something)."

Believe it or not, this 1450 definition is indicated as "rare or obsolete."

In any event, the 1430 definition, carrying the distinction of "superior understanding" seems to have served until some point after 1882 after which scientific research of intelligence entered the picture.

It is quite clear that the research began under the auspices of certain pre-fixed ideas, one of which was based on the notion of so-called natural superior and natural inferior forms of intelligence.

Thus, when the term INTELLIGENTSIA came into use (roughly between 1900 and 1914), its meaning was drawn from a Russian word defined as "The class of society to which culture, superior intelligence, and advanced political views are attributed."

This indicates that the matter of intelligence (as understanding) had been converted into societal uses and functions, within which the major definition had to do with "the capacity to apprehend facts and propositions and their relations and to reason about them."

Well, yes, such is probably an aspect of intelligence. But common observation will reveal that reason and reasoning can take place often in the absence not only of too much understanding, but also the absence of too many facts and proportions.

Furthermore, the definition above almost surely requires the interfacing of educational training, the auspices of which have never been equally distributed throughout all social class levels.

In any event, one of the early modern "psychological" definitions of intelligence appeared roughly between 1900 and 1920, to wit:

> "In psychology, the general mental ability involved in calculating, reasoning, perceiving relationships and analogies, learning quickly, storing and retrieving information, using language fluently, classifying, generalizing, and adjusting to new situations."

Some version of this modernist definition has held social and cultural sway ever since. And so it is herewith useful to contrast it to the definitions of UNDERSTANDING. In most dictionaries, these are given as:

> "Discernment, insight; the power of comprehending, specifically the general capacity to apprehend general relations of particulars; the power to make experience intelligible by applying concepts and categories; the power of having knowledge and judgment."

Anyone interested in empowerment might wish to meditate, at some length, on the definitions of these two terms. Both are applicable to intelligence, of course. But in the end, it will be observed that one of the definitions is quantitative, the other being qualitative.

Furthermore, one benefits largely from artificially acquired education programming -- whereas the other is more akin to being innate and spontaneously present.

Most sources recounting the more modern history of research into intelligence generally end up indicating that "the concept of intelligence has proved to be so elusive that psychologists often prefer to define it as that which is measured by intelligence tests."

Here, however, it might be considered that intelligence is NOT a concept but is most certainly an innate power.

EVOLUTION OF MODERNIST IQ TESTS

While no consensus of opinion prevails about what "intelligence tests" actually measure, their use in education has had great practical value.

Indeed, throughout most of the twentieth century, IQ tests were conducted and broadly utilized in three categories of social management processes:

A "practical" method of assigning high or low mental intelligent quotients to individuals;

A "practical" method of segmenting and adjudicating societal planning experiments;

A "practical" method of overt and covert societal management systems.

During the last two decades of the twentieth century, however, the value and meaning of IQ tests began to undergo strong and eventually devastating criticism via some cutting-edge researchers of intelligence -- especially in respect to the usage of intelligence as social ideology.

As some researchers have pointed out, intelligence has probably been an active carrier of social ideology for as long as social classes have existed, and the preservation of privilege has remained an ideological imperative.

As Ken Richardson (whose book was mentioned earlier) has pointed out, in the nineteenth century Britain underwent renewed stress at home and throughout the Empire regarding the long-enduring concept of "natural inequality," and which stress led "to the invention of the IQ test."

According to Richardson, Britain's proponents of "natural inequality" argued strongly that "the minds of the inferior human races could not respond to relations of even moderate complexity," and that "the poor, having thus proved themselves to be 'unfit', should be denied all social welfare and normal reproduction, and be allowed to die off."

Richardson goes on to point up that the founders of the intelligence-testing movement in the United States and Britain "were mostly strong hereditarians and eugenicists, who saw the IQ test as the key instrument in promoting their cause."

One of the functions of IQ tests in societal terms was that they revealed natural, and possibly genetic, differences between those of high and low IQ scores.

Obviously, IQ scores seen that way helped to justify the societal power structure picture of the "natural" divisions between superior and inferior intelligence.

In that picture, the naturally superior intelligence genetic elite effortlessly ascended to positions of power and privilege in society, while those of naturally inferior intelligence constituted nothing more than a genetic underclass.

This gross usage of IQ tests did undergo softening during the 1950s. Even so, many studies have shown how knowledge of low IQ scores has contributed to low self-esteem and has contributed to reduced aspirations and long-term damage to self-confidence among large populations.

Furthermore, debate about IQ testing has contributed to many kinds of social despair about so-called "natural" inferiority and has produced various kinds of fatalism about the human species in general.

INTELLIGENCE AS AN INNATE HUMAN POWER THAT LARGELY REMAINS NON-NURTURED AND UNTAPPED

One of the reasons for dragging through the foregoing is to be able to point out several nuances that are never mentioned in connection with the problems of intelligence.

It is difficult to see how the human species could continue as such if the majority of individuals possess naturally inferior formats of intelligence.

It is far easier to consider that every individual born of the species possesses innate powers of intelligence, but that those innate powers do not undergo societal nurturing.

Innate intelligence powers probably require the activation of a number of subsidiary powers in order to function at various levels of awareness and perception, and if some of those subsidiary powers are inactive, then the sum of intellectual power will not function too well.

In that sense, it is interesting to consider what intelligence IS, but it is also to be wondered what powers contribute to and enhance its functioning.

Chapter 11

ENERGIES OF MIND

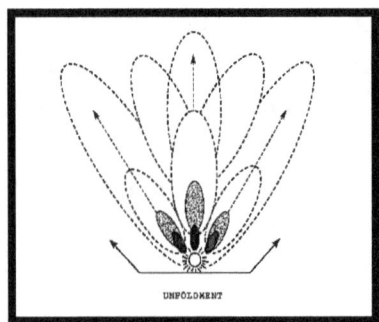

PROFOUND THINKERS in the distant and recent past have generally held that the mind is all that counts.

One finds it difficult to argue against this. But the statement really could be amended to read that the POWERS of the mind are all that count.

It is quite difficult to think that a mind that does not have powers IS a mind -- and if this is hard to grok, one should try thinking of one's mind without its having powers. It is NOT possible for a mind to exist and not have its powers, because they are the same thing in any practical sense.

As has been pointed out earlier, power(s) of mind are not considered as a part(s) of the mind. And so there is some small sense of satisfaction in restoring the powers collective (the power spectrum) as an inseparable part of mind.

However, there is a more fundamental part that needs to be considered, a part, which, surprisingly, has hardly ever been considered before.

Like the entire human organism, it is quite clear that the mind is an energy-driven apparatus that needs either the equivalent of "batteries" in order to function, or some manner of deriving energy from wherever it does.

It is quite simple to establish this energy factor as a full and legitimate part of mind, because most recognize, perhaps even experience, what happens when the needed energy is low, non-existent, or ceases altogether.

For increased clarity here, it is now necessary to further elaborate on what is stated just above.

THE POWER PART OF MIND

As discussed in Volume I, it is possible that individuals can be selectively educated and socially conditioned so as to become unaware that minds have powers.

In such a situation, mind and its powers can exist, but one can be unaware of some or most of the powers - and, as well, perhaps be unaware of some or most of one's mind overall.

In any event, mind inclusive of its powers, is clearly one of the principal factors that must be included with respect to overall emergence and unfoldment of empowerment.

THE ENERGY PART OP MIND

Most already realize the foregoing, of course. What might not be generally realized is that the idea of mind and its powers is virtually USELESS unless the concepts of vital energy and force are added into it.

The idea of mental energy is not unknown, to be sure. What is strange is that mental energy can be thought of as energy expended in thinking activity -- but with little or no realization that mind ITSELF is an energy -- based "machine," so to speak.

This can be somewhat elaborated by suggesting that mind and its powers are vital energy-based systems -- and that without the energy basis, the multiple power components of the systems will not function.

The exact nature of this energy basis is not at all understood, except that it is at least akin to some kind of electrical activity.

But what is understood, especially among ostensible mind-controllers, is that mind energy can be vitalized and/or devitalized -- which is to say, nurtured and empowered, or depowered and deadened.

The most amazing factor of all is that mind-energy-powers can be artificially shaped by information-knowledge inputs, and by withholding them.

In other words, information-knowledge inputs awaken and unfold energy-mind-powers activity -- while, with some few exceptions, an absence of information-knowledge inputs does not.

The result of the shaping, of course, more or less equates to social conditioning and resulting reality boxes -- and which means that any and all kinds of reality boxes can be formatted depending on knowledge provided or withheld.

Chapter 12

THE SUBCONSCIOUS PART OF MIND

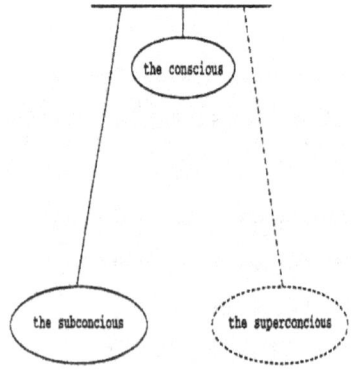

AS MENTIONED in chapter 8, while most individuals have not been exposed to too many parts of the mind, there is one part that has achieved wide and even notorious worldwide visibility via books, media, and psychology, and so almost everyone has at least heard of it.

This is the SUBCONSCIOUS part, whose existence is generally accepted, but the functions and processes of which are yet a matter of great and on-going debates.

One reason for the debates is that the subconscious part seems to have, of all things, powers of its own, many of which are extraordinary when evidence of them can be seen.

Anything that can be seen as having powers of its own becomes a matter of alarmed concern, even with respect to the human individual level, and to the mind itself.

Of course, the best conventional way, at the societal levels, to contain and soothe this alarm is not to admit into evidence whatever demonstrates powers of its own, and especially not what the powers are.

The "discovery" of the subconscious constitutes a modern affair mostly focused within the early decades of the twentieth century. The discovery, and expositions of it, caused what can only be called panics in science, sociology, and elsewhere.

Those panics, and their potentially culture-shaping magnitudes, have been quelled and forgotten -- but only because conventional sciences and associated professions managed to install rather harmless and boring definitions for the subconscious. To wit: in psychology, especially of the Freudian type, the subconscious is defined as "a transition zone through which repressed material must pass on its way from the unconscious to consciousness."

In psychiatry, the same is defined as "partial unconsciousness, also the state in which mental processes take place without conscious perception on the subject's part."

Of course, subliminal researchers have more impressive definitions for the subconscious, but conventional societal professions contain and curtail these definitions by excluding them and the subliminal researchers from any of the societal realms of authenticity.

The term SUBCONSCIOUS was actually coined about 1832 by Thomas de Quincy (1785-1859), who was one of the first to intellectually explore the mind-altering effects of opium.

By 1882, two non-conventional, but slightly contradictory, definitions had been established for the term: (1) Partially or imperfectly conscious; belonging to a class of phenomena resembling consciousness, but not clearly perceived or recognized by it; (2) Belonging to that portion of the mental field the processes of which are outside the range of attention.

And, it might be added, not completely outside the range of sensing and experiencing as many have come to realize.

In any event, one can examine numerous clinical definitions of subconscious without encountering too much information about what it DOES.

Very good short descriptions of what the subconscious does were included by the writer Robert Collier in his book THE SECRET OF THE AGES, published in 1948, but who mostly quotes sources published late in the nineteenth century.

Some of those descriptions are included herewith because they have stood the tests of time, because they are clearly put and uncluttered, and because they stipulate the existence of certain important powers of mind.

As Collier wrote:

"The subconscious mind is a distinct entity. It occupies the whole of the human body, and, when not opposed in any way, it has absolute control over all the functions, conditions, and sensations of the body.

"While the objective (conscious) mind has control over all of our voluntary functions and motions, the subconscious mind controls all of the silent, involuntary, and vegetative functions.

"Nutrition, waste, all secretions and excretions, the action of the heart in circulation of the blood, the lungs in respiration or breathing, and all cell life, cell changes and development, are positively under the complete control of the subconscious mind.

"This was the only mind animals had before the evolution of the brain; and it could not, nor can it yet, reason inductively, but its power of deductive reasoning is perfect.

"It is this mind that carries on the work of assimilation and up building whilst we sleep. It reveals to us things that the conscious mind has no conception of until the consummations have occurred. It gets glimpses of things that ordinary sight does not behold. It warns of approaching danger.

"And more, it can see without the use of physical eyes. It perceives by intuition. It has the power to communicate with others without the aid of the ordinary physical means.

> "It can read the thoughts of others. It receives intelligence [i.e., information] and transmits it to people at a distance. Distance offers no resistance against the successful missions of the subconscious mind."

One of the most interesting aspects of this description of the subconscious part of the mind is the clear reference to the powers of telepathy, intuition, and clairvoyance.

These powers are of course lopped off and deleted from most modern maps of the mind, largely because societal power structures would rather not encourage ANY knowledge of their existence and have thus propagandized against them throughout the modernist decades.

However, as will be discussed shortly, it is now scientifically understood that the human body possesses receptors for telepathic information, as well as for other kinds of information having very distant sources.

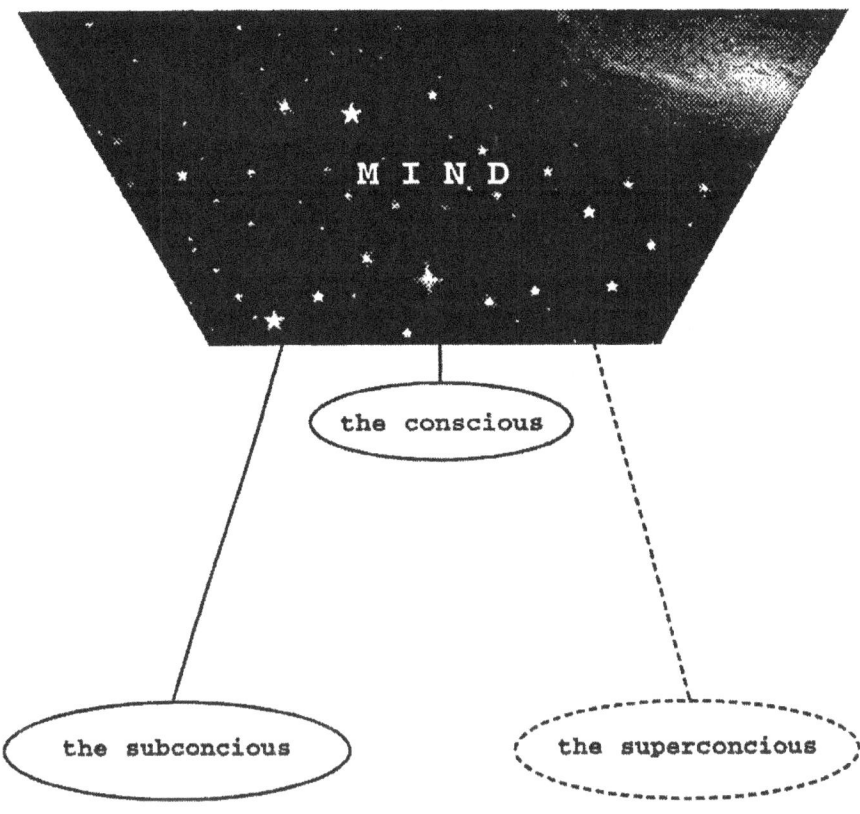

FIGURE 6. The principal, two-part concept of Mind most conventionally favored during the 20th century. The existence of a "superconscious" part has been suggested by some researchers. But the existence of that part has not yet been accepted into conventional mainstream reality, although it has been of deep interest in non-mainstream considerations. One reason for the non-acceptance is that while the conscious and subconscious parts can be considered as "internal" to the biological body, the superconscious part suggests that mind has functions that extend beyond the perhipheries of the physical body.

Chapter 13

THE CONSCIOUS PART OF MIND AND ITS SURFACE ENERGIES

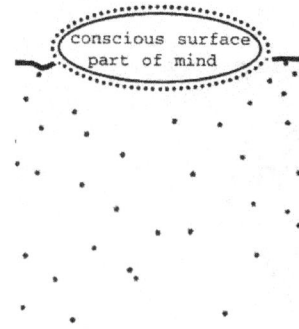

WHATEVER PARTS the Blind may or may not have, it does have an aspect referred to in modernist times as the conscious part.

It is awkward to discuss this part because the term CONSCIOUSNESS is now used in so many contexts that it has become ambiguous and confusing.

For example, it is often said that the mind is capable of very many natural or altered states of consciousness which the conscious part is not usually, if ever, conscious of.

If one can understand this, all the better. If not, the fault is not one's own, but arises from a lack of a more extensive and precise vocabulary that has yet to evolve.

Nevertheless, the conscious part of the mind can be identified more or less precisely because it is generally conceptualized as what one experiences while one is awake.

The term CONSCIOUS is taken from the Latin COM + SCIRE which literally means "with + to know" or "with knowing."

In modern English, this is refined and elaborated as "perceiving, apprehending, or noticing with a degree of controlled thought or observation while awake and aware."

In other words, the conscious part of the mind consists of the awake state that everyone automatically utilizes in going about their daily activities the best they can -- albeit doing so within the contexts of what they know and what they don't know.

There is no doubt that the conscious part of the mind is crucial and of enormous importance. And so it is usually thought of in general as a big part of the mind, perhaps the biggest, and having dominion over all other aspects or parts of the mind. However, it can easily be shown that the conscious part of the mind is its smallest part when compared with the subconscious part that is thought to occupy approximately 90 percent of the entire mind-package.

So, when individuals make active use only of their conscious mind part, they are using but a fraction of their mind-package.

It is important to consider this for a very specific reason.

While in the active awake state, the conscious part of the mind tends to focus on whatever it does via the five physical senses.

These five senses are of utmost importance, of course. They majorly scan the surfaces of whatever they do perceive -- and it is quite certain that they cannot scan whatever is beneath the surfaces of things, or beyond their ranges of perception.

Furthermore, the conscious part apparently functions, to a large degree anyway, with respect to what it can recognize and become aware of.

Many kinds of awareness must be nurtured and learned, and if this nurturing and learning does not take place, then the activities of the conscious part can be quite limited even if they seem sufficient.

As discussed in Volume I, most social and societal frameworks do not in general encourage nurturing of awareness because doing so will begin the processes of empowerment among the subservient masses.

It is therefore convenient to societal power structures that the masses continue to dwell within the limited contexts of surface perceptions and issues -- and, to be sure, within the contexts of surface energies, as it were.

Not all individuals are limited to 10 percent contexts of the conscious awake mind. But many are, even without realizing it, and are content to run on low gear all their lives -- to function only in the contexts of surface energies.

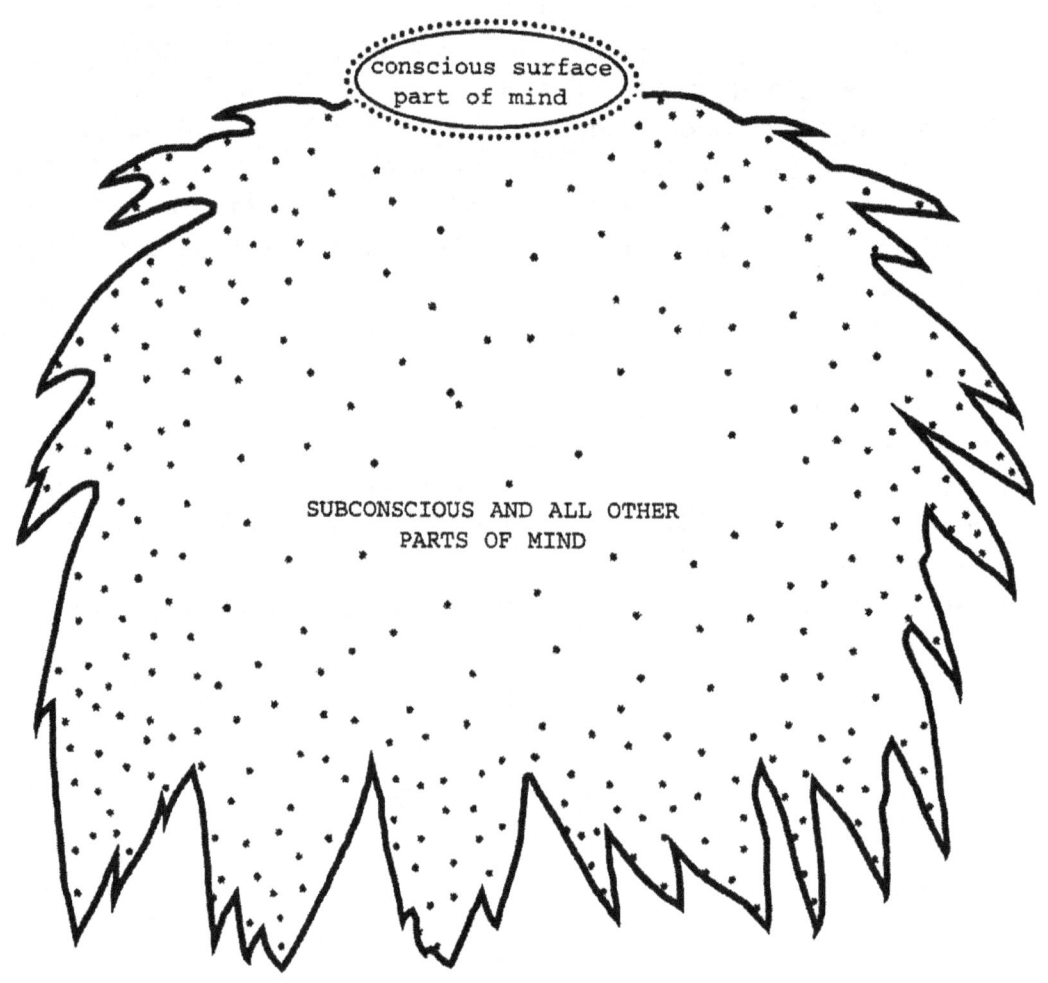

FIGURE 7. It is roughly estimated that the conscious part of mind comprises, on average, only about 10 percent of the entire mind, while the subconscious part comprises all the rest of it, and whose contents and mechanisms are held to be inaccessible to the conscious part. The conscious part refers to the general and routine awake state that individuals use on a daily basis to interact with physical environments. But it might include slightly altered states of consciousness experienced while awake and active. While this 10 percent concept is actual enough on average, it is unsuited to the whole of the mind that is, of course, marvelously complex. What the 10 percent concept is best suited for is social conditioning that works to depress more extensive conscious awareness, especially awareness beyond physicality.

Chapter 14

THE STRENGTH-OF-POWER(S) PART OF MIND

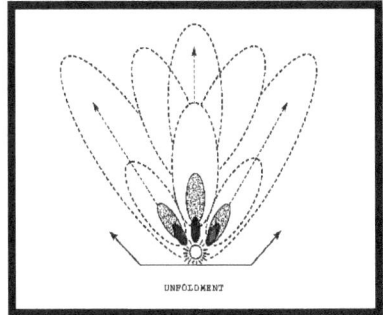

THERE ARE many hopeful approaches for achieving empowerment, and one of these begins with the idea that one must know what power IS, as a thing-in-itself, before one can begin to develop it in self.

This idea of what something is seems logical enough, because it is obviously applicable to so many other endeavors. So there have been many discussions about what power is, and all of which, some of which, or none of which contain pertinent information.

For the purposes of this volume, however, it can be observed that whatever power may be, it manifests on a gradient scale ranging from weak to strong, or, perhaps, from inferior to superior.

Therefore, the concept of em-powerment (gain of power) is self-suggestive of movement along this scale from a weak power status toward a stronger one.

Likewise, the concept of de-powerment (loss of power) is self-suggestive of movement toward a weaker or an inferior power status.

In a general sense, the question of what power is always involves the situational relationships of the many things and factors among which power manifests on the weak-to-strong scale.

But few will attribute power to weak-power, but only to stronger manifestations of it.

So power must stick out, so to speak, as strong in order for it to be recognized as power.

In the sense of the above, then, whatever power is, it must be strong enough to be identified, recognized, and accepted as power. And it is for this reason that the standard dictionary definitions of the word STRENGTH become important.

- The quality or state of being strong;
- Capacity for exertion or endurance;
- Power to resist force;
- Power of resisting attack;
- Intensity and vigor of expression or action.

The standard definitions of strength (and "strong") are usually associated with great or robust physical power, although they are equally applicable to other factors that are inherent in individual human systems, and which are commonly described as "powers."

One can refer to physical strength and physical powers, yet the human is not made up of only the physical. Indeed, for a human to be fully considered as human, our species' powers of mind must be entered into the picture.

While it might seem rather silly to point out this obvious factor, it becomes important in the contexts of depowerment -- and which contexts are always as important as those of empowerment.

As seen throughout Volume I of this series, powers of mind can be depowered by reducing them into a weakened or dormant state. When, therefore, one thinks in terms of empowerment, one is thinking in terms of shifting powers of mind from their weakened condition into a strengthened state.

The best way to depower powers of mind is to keep knowledge of them in a confused or ambiguous state via this or that societal confabulation -- even keeping exact descriptions of them in states of "secrecy" so that their nature and functions are inaccessible and cannot be learned about.

A full part of this approach to empowerment thus entails learning about what powers of mind actually consist of. This is easy enough to do regarding some of the many factors involved. But there are other factors that are more difficult to identify.

There is a "bottom line" here. One cannot empower (strengthen) what one cannot identify.

Chapter 15

THE POWER NUCLEUS PART OF MIND

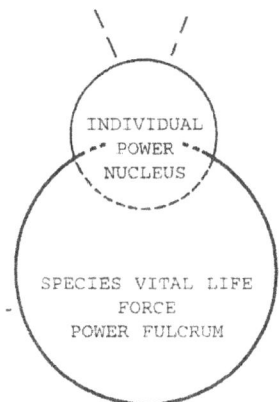

MANY WHO feel powerless or relatively powerless can, in some sense at least, feel embarrassed by their condition.

As a result, some develop various kinds of attitudes against power itself -- for example, attitudes of resentment, anger, disdain, and so forth.

And above all, many can come to feel that the fault is somehow theirs alone and are thereafter further wrecked by their feelings of self-power inferiority.

Generally speaking, though, such feelings come about via sources external to the individual, sources that fail to nurture indwelling powers as much as possible in as many as possible.

The whole of this constitutes a terribly complex issue. It is also one of those crucial problems that never gets presented in ways that can be understood.

The complexity plus the general absence of understanding permit much to be swept under rugs and into closed and forbidden categories of human potentials.

And it is this, in turn, that permits societal power structures to simply roll over, without too much bother, the loss of empowerment of the actual majority of our species.

The whole of the foregoing is, of course, a negative issue, with the implication that any suggestive way to correct or change it is to overthrow and pull down the societal power structures involved.

Indeed, our history reflects many such overthrowing activities, sometimes not by the aggregate powerless themselves, but even within the competitive camps of the powerful.

The historical experience, however, clearly shows that a new power structure is always ready to replace an old one, and that the new is something of a carbon copy of what was replaced.

And so, as the old axiom goes, everything might change, but everything remains the same.

The reason for trolling through the foregoing negative scenario is to establish grounds for pointing up an empowerment factor that is implicit in it, although seldom recognized.

If individuals did not have innate powers, then it is difficult to comprehend why they should feel their absence.

It is also difficult to comprehend why power structure arrangements seek to establish depowerment methodologies to dumb down something that does not exist in the targeted populations.

Generally speaking, and all other factors considered, one cannot feel powerless unless one senses, even if only minimally, that one has innate powers that are there, but are inactive, deadened, or not operational.

And in observable fact, one cannot achieve control over the powers of others, unless the others have powers to be controlled.

In this sense, it can happen that the powerless feel powerless because they sense or comprehend that they possess powers, but the activation of which has been subordinated to those having achieved power superiority.

And it is the foregoing consideration that opens up perception regarding the central topic of this chapter, i.e., what DO the powerless sense in general that makes them feel powerless in general?

In the first instance here, it is reasonable to assume that the powerless might feel powerless because of installed ignorance about the nature of power, kinds of power, and power machinations in particular, and especially because of the controlled denial of empowerment to them.

Certainly, everyone experiencing such things can sense factors inherent in power control systems.

Such factors actually arise from sources external to the individual, not from within individuals themselves -- and the sensing of such external factors can indeed increase feelings of powerlessness.

But if the powerless did not sense some power source internal to themselves, then they might feel put upon by external demands, but not necessarily feel powerless of and in themselves.

While such may not be applicable in all cases of felt powerlessness, it can be thought that feelings of self-powerlessness occur because one feels that one has power sources within self, even though their activation and development have been thwarted by external factors.

In one respect, the powerless do not know what their powers are; otherwise they might not be so powerless.

Yet the internal presence of a power source can be felt, even if one does not know what it consists of, and the defeat of that power source can be felt as well.

The concept of a power source is often used without too much exactness. Even so, it automatically transliterates into the concept of an energy source.

As has been discussed earlier, the terms power and energy are used as synonyms. But energy is defined as a capacity, potential or otherwise, to produce "work," while power is defined as the ability to act or produce an effect or result of some kind.

In other words, power can be thought of as directed energy, as compared to energy that is not being directed, but which exists as potential.

It is one of the innate powers of our species, and of all its individuals, to feel the presence of energy (i.e., of potential), and this takes place at several different levels of human sensing systems.

But it is also possible to feel feeling without intellectually or consciously being able to identify what the feeling involves in its particulars.

It is thus also possible to feel energy or energies without being able consciously to identify or specify the particulars involved (and which, of course, requires specific concepts and a vocabulary to do so).

This is the same as saying that the powerless will feel the presence of the energies involved, even though they might not be able to conceptually identify their powers.

Indeed, all powers can be recognized as directed or dynamic extensions of the energies fundamentally necessary to effect activations of them.

In this sense, although they can be thought of in many different ways, all individuals really do have to be fundamentally thought of as energy modules, or something like that -- for if they were to be energy-less, then they would be dead.

It is via these considerations that we trip across a great mystery. Human beings are conceptualized via many different images of them, and many different Images of Man have been conceptualized in the past.

Whatever the image involved, human beings at base are not only life forms, but also energetic life forms, and this is completely beyond question.

Yet, neither the human species nor its downloaded individuals are ever referred to that way, and, most precisely, are NOT conceptualized as energy life entities, or as bio-mind energy life forms.

But this is the same as saying that each individual is an innate energy-power entity BEFORE it is possible to become anything else, anything additional, anything evolutional or creational, or anything mutational or transfigurative.

In fact, although it is very daring to say as much, the human being-entity is an energy-power package BEFORE its DNA genetic sequencing can become operational.

If one meditates upon the essences of the foregoing observations, it can become obvious that some sort of centralizing concept is missing from the Image of Man thing -- a concept that introduces the all-important reality of "Man" as energy-power modules.

THE ENERGY-POWER NUCLEUS

In modern times, the best-known definition of NUCLEUS is the biological one that, with variations, can be found in most dictionaries as:

"A portion of cell protoplasm held to be essential to vital phenomena and heredity, made up of a network rich in nucleoproteins from which chromosomes and nucleoli arise and a hyaline grouped substance, and enclosed by a definite membrane."

However, NUCLEUS is taken from a Latin term, defined as "kernel or inner part," into English at about 1702, and was first utilized in astronomy of the time to refer to "the head of a comet."

At about 1762, it was given larger definition as:

"A central part or thing around which other parts or things are grouped, collected, or compacted; that which forms the center or kernel of some aggregate or mass."

These definitions are useful -- until it comes to wondering just WHY "other parts or things" should become "grouped, collected, or compacted" around "a central part or thing." After all, there has to be some sort of, as it were, organizational logic involved.

And, with regard to the modernist biological definition, one might also wonder what is meant by the phrase "vital phenomena."

These wonderings are of real interest to any seeking empowerment -- or, more frankly put, getting more power.

And, indeed, if the 1762 definition of nucleus is meditated upon, it can easily be observed that it is also one of the most central definitions of human power, not only with respect to the societal power structure kind, but also to any other kinds of power.

Just about everyone will know what the term VITAL means, even without consulting dictionaries. The reason is that they usually know it when they see or encounter something that manifests as such.

The term VITALITY, however, has three principal definitions that are more directly to the point:

1. The peculiarity that distinguishes the living from the nonliving.
2. The capacity to live and develop; also, physical and mental vigor, especially when highly developed.
3. The power of enduring or continuing.

Here again we trip across yet another sensible definition of power -- to live, to develop, and enduring and continuing as what is developed.

The essence of the foregoing is surely a matter well known, a matter of common sense, even to the degree of being a trite platitude.

But it becomes less platitudinous if one begins to wonder if to live, to develop, and to endure can take place in the absence of energy plus powers.

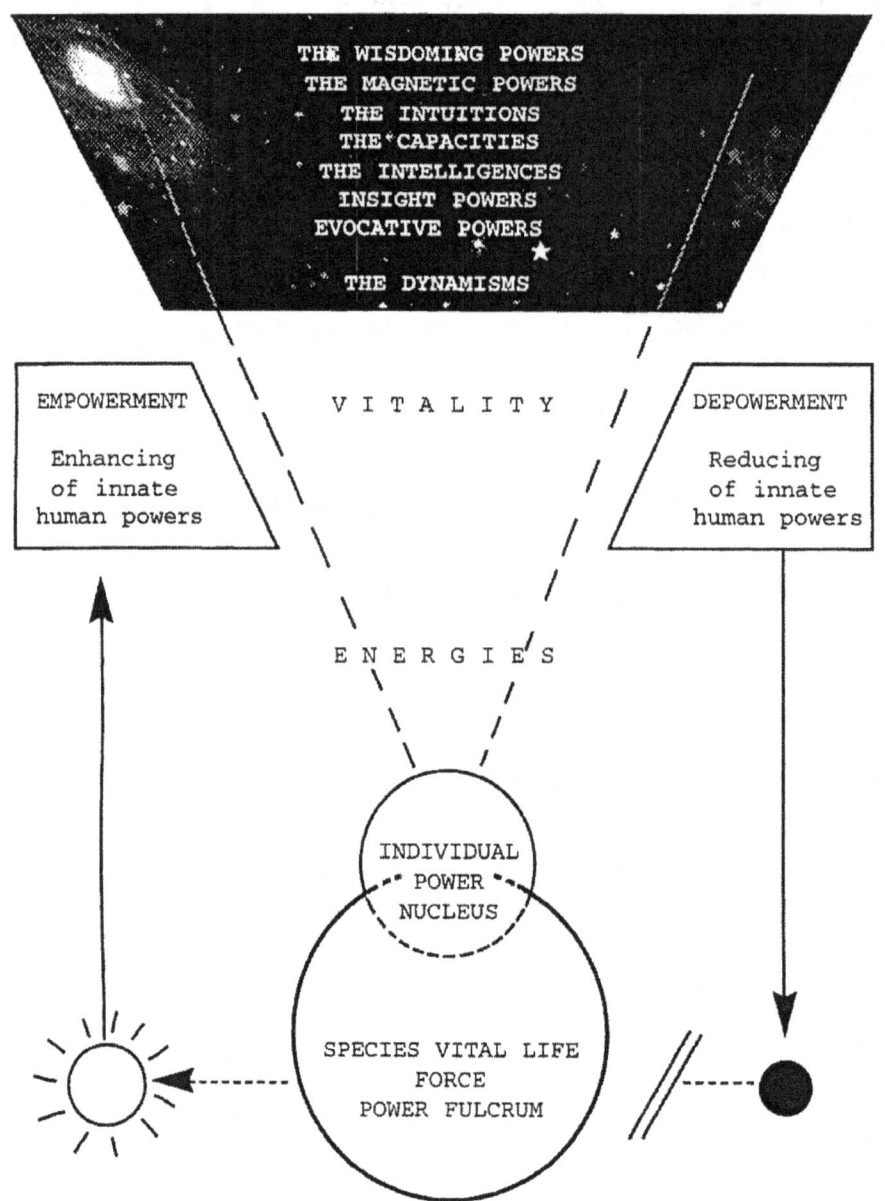

FIGURE 8. This schematic represents just one concept regarding human empowering energies, but only if elements of depowerment are considered as real as those of empowerment. The processes of depowerment are the least examined of all human phenomena, but if they are not recognized as such then there is no real scale by which to measure and realize empowerment. Individuals interested in achieving some kind of empowerment might attempt to make additional schematics of their own.

PART THREE
POSSIBLE ROUTES FOR ENTERING EMPOWERMENT AT THE INDIVIDUAL LEVEL

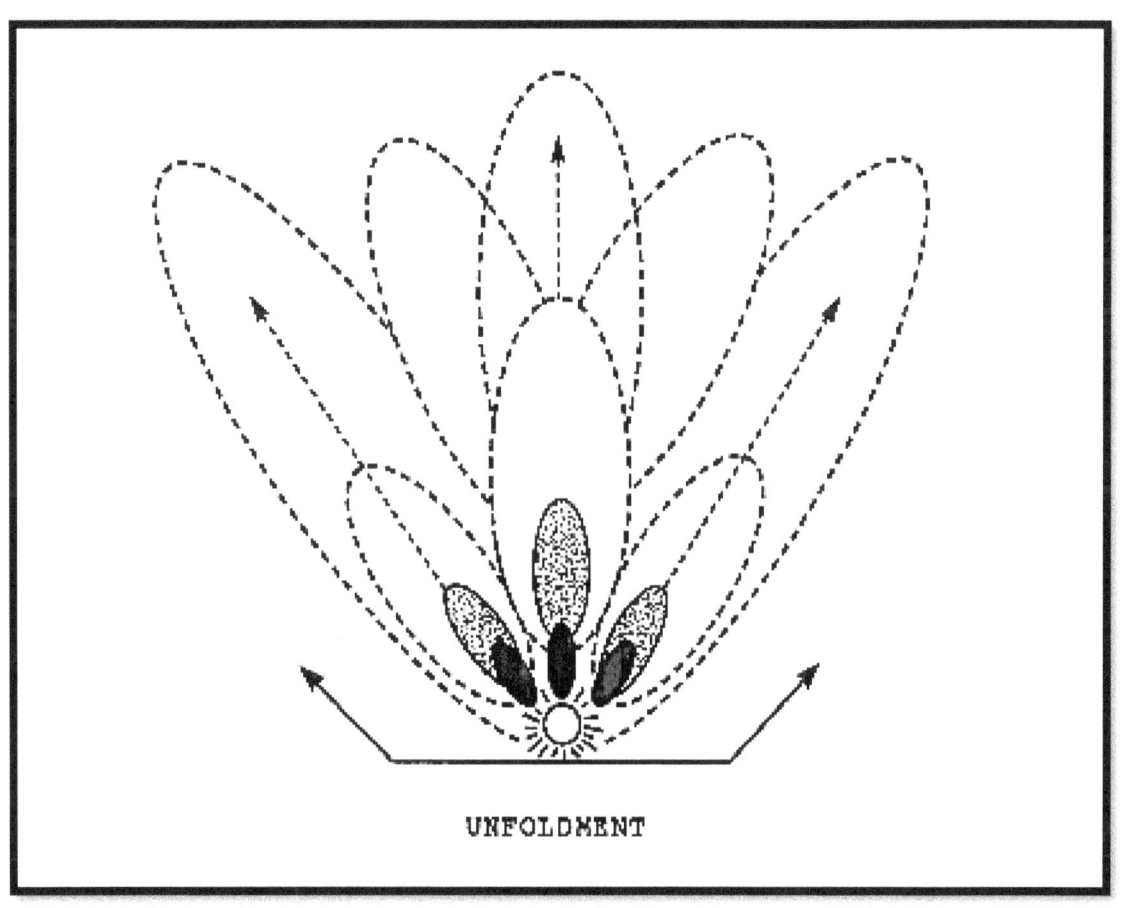

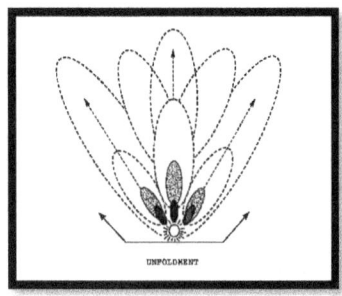

Chapter 16

EMPOWERMENT VIA REALITY BOX RETOOLING

IT IS not possible to estimate what given individuals might think empowerment can consist of, because all individuals have their particular sets of realities. Thus, what works for some may not work for others.

In general, empowerment suggests undergoing a change of power functioning on a scale ranging from no or little power to more and more of it. So, no matter what kinds of reality boxes are involved, the concept of change of power functioning is probably relevant across the boards.

The word ROUTE refers to "means of access," while PATHWAY is defined as "a track specially constructed for a particular use."

Thus, the concept of "entering" into empowerment implies the locating of means of access into empowerment phenomena, and thereafter constructing power functioning pathways that are relevant to given reality boxes.

The whole of this can more or less be conceptualized as retooling one's reality boxes by acquiring whatever information packages are needed to energize them more in the direction of arousing energetic power function increases.

The principal difficulty in thinking along such lines is the absence of knowledge that individuals have innate powers that can be turned off and on -- principally because of influencing situations and circumstances external to them, and which they have adapted to.

Such influencing situations and circumstances can be thought of as constituting various kinds of reality boxes, within which exist social criteria regarding what is to be nurtured or not, and which criteria individuals likewise adapt to.

And here again arises the issue of socio-cultural reality boxes that influence the reality awareness of so many individuals.

Individuals can seek to support or reject various kinds of reality boxes, and, as pointed out earlier, much of human history has reflected just this kind of activity throughout the ages. In this sense, human history is composed of endless contests between various kinds of reality boxes.

But there are two factors about reality boxes that seem never to have been identified.

First, all reality boxes constitute operative mind maps of some kind, even if inadequately formatted.

Second, that so many reality boxes can be formatted anywhere, everywhere, and in all times and ages, is entirely suggestive of the inescapable fact that formatting them does constitute a very important human power innate in our species.

If such is the case, then that power downloads into each individual of the species as an innate potential, and which potential undergoes influencing and shaping by the specifications and criteria within situations and circumstances external to the individual.

This is the same as saying that humans can make reality boxes because they have the innate power to do so.

If this is the case, then the innate power is senior to whatever end product in any given time or place is thence formatted or not formatted.

As will be discussed ahead, reality boxes seem to be formatted almost exactly in pace with whatever each individual becomes both aware and not aware of.

And here, finally, is something familiar and recognizable, for it is generally understood and accepted that increases of awareness nurture reality box re-tooling and restructuring.

It is in this sense that becoming aware of what one's innate powers are needs to take place before the powers can become active enough to be extended outward into the situations and circumstances external to the individual.

After all, if one does not know what one's powers are, it can be quite difficult to "enter" some kind of empowerment into them.

SUGGESTED RESEARCH

TRY TO OBSERVE THE REALITY BOXES OF OTHERS, ESPECIALLY WITH REGARD TO LIMITATIONS AND WHAT MAY BE MISSING IN THEM IT IS ADVISABLE NOT TO DISCUSS THESE OBSERVATIONS

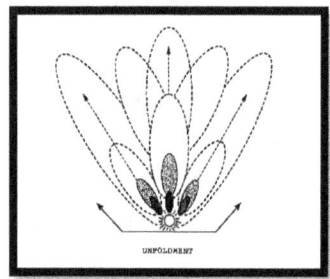

Chapter 17

EMPOWERMENT VIA THE STUDY OF DEPOWERMENT

IN THE light of the several foregoing discussions, it would be obvious that any human power transmuted from a turned-off to a turned-on state could be employed within the contexts of societal reality boxes.

And, as discussed throughout Volume I, it would also be obvious that pyramidal power structures function best when a number of human powers are turned off within the larger, more inclusive, individual levels.

The concepts of "to empower" and "to enable" are largely synonymous, since both mean "to make one able to do something."

The opposite concepts, however, are "to disable" and "to depower," which are not exactly synonymous.

To DISABLE implies interfering with, or sabotaging, something so that it doesn't work too well, or stops working altogether.

To DEPOWER, however, carries the concept of reducing the power, force, energy, strength, or might of something. In this sense, to POWER UP and to POWER DOWN are the more workable contexts regarding human powers.

To most individuals, and generally speaking, empowerment means to power up, with very little interest directed toward identifying and realizing what has been powered down or disabled.

In this sense, the assumption seems to be that positive empowerment will automatically negate or overcome negative depowerment -- and so there is no apparent reason to examine how depowerment is made to occur.

Well, it might come as a surprise to discover that this assumption is entirely consistent with the workings of most societal power structures in which it is very important that the methods and mechanisms of depowerment should NOT be brought to light.

The identifiable reason for this is that if those methods and mechanisms become broadly identifiable, then more individuals can escape from them.

The general axiom here seems to be: empower self if one can, but never look to discover the methods and mechanisms of depowerment.

Indeed, even if a few achieve some kind of self-empowerment, it is more important, in the larger societal power sense, that large-scale depowerment remains in place. This guarantees that the masses of the relatively powerless will continue to exist as such and continue in their subservient condition.

One needs only to reflect upon the concepts of the empowered mind and the depowered mind to come closer to what is involved.

As many writers have noted, power structures are held together by the various mechanisms of social conditioning. For example, John Kenneth Galbraith points this up in his valuable book.

THE ANATOMY OF POWER (1983)

However, what exactly social conditioning consists of is usually not gone into at any depth -- because the actual mechanisms of the condition are seldom brought into open inspection.

But the goal of social conditioning is broadly acknowledged as bringing into existence a population that is receptive, acceptive, and submissive with respect to the power structure.

There may be many ways and means to achieve such populations. One of the major ways is to withhold information and knowledge that might bring about unwanted shifts with respect to the desired receptive, acceptive, and submissive characteristics of the population.

It is thus that if one examines the reality boxes of most societal power structures, it can become apparent that few of them contain information and knowledge about the ways and means of depowerment.

This clearly means that those who have adapted to the societal reality boxes will have adapted to reality boxes that do not contain open information and knowledge about depowerment.

One might therefore think that societal depowerment does NOT exist, and that one has never been an unwitting victim to it.

There are two reasons why methods and mechanisms of depowerment are hidden. The first, of course, has to do with elements of social conditioning. The second has to do with the fact that the more one knows about depowerment, the more one will know about empowerment.

Indeed, if depowerment can be recognized, then it becomes obvious what can be empowered -- and this is of major assistance with regard to individual empowerment efforts. Many cannot recognize in self what has been depowered, because if they could do so then empowerment would have already commenced.

Beyond recognizing the existence of totally depowered minds, it is far easier at first to observe what powers in particular may have been depowered in others.

SUGGESTED EXERCISE

TRY TO IDENTIFY EXAMPLES OF DEPOWERMENT REGARDING OTHERS, AND, POSSIBLY, HOW THE DEPOWERMENT HAS COME ABOUT BEAR IN MIND THAT PEOPLE DO NOT LIKE TO THINK THEY HAVE BEEN DEPOWERED, SO AVOID DISCUSSION THIS IS JUST AN EXERCISE

Chapter 18

EMPOWERMENT VIA THE PRINCIPLE OF UNFOLDMENT

Empowerment via reality box retooling

Empowerment via the study of depowerment

Empowerment via the principle of unfoldment

Empowerment via enhancing human senses and perception

THE IMPORTANT topic of unfoldment has been presented and discussed throughout chapter 23 of Volume I. The purpose of reintroducing the topic in this chapter is to make a few extensions within the contexts of individual empowerment.

As was pointed out, the verb UNFOLD is not usually applied to the contexts of power and empowerment.

For convenience here, the term is defined as:
- To open the folds of;
- To spread out, expand, open up;
- To open to view;
- To make clear by gradual disclosure;
- To blossom;
- To develop by increasing or expanding; to gradually make clear to understanding.

The fourth definition above can be amended to read: "To make clear by gradual disclosure, or by gradual increases of awareness."

As discussed earlier, one cannot deal with whatever one is unaware of, and so the aware/unaware equation has a great deal to do with any individual attempt at empowerment.

Indeed, it can be said that empowerment is basically a problem involving a contraction or expansion of awareness.

It can also be said that depowerment consists of preventing, reducing, or cutting back of awareness, and since this is so, empowerment consists of reinstating, enlarging, and adding more awareness to one's overall thresholds of same.

It can easily be recognized that preventing or reducing awareness would work toward turning off perceptions of whatever is involved. And if perceptions are turned off, then numerous effects of power downsizing will naturally occur.

It can also be seen that the aware/unaware equation has a great deal to do not only with the expansion and contraction of empowerment, but with whether the principle of unfoldment will be active or inactive in given individuals in given areas of their mental equipment.

For more clarity, the principle of unfoldment rests upon the two-fold reality that there is something that can undergo unfoldment, and that the something is naturally prepackaged to unfold.

The analogy most frequently utilized for this is the seed which when planted will gradually unfold into the tree -- IF nurturing conditions are present for it to do so.

In the case of the human, the egg and sperm have been referred to as "seeds" that combine to produce or reproduce another human.

More fundamentally speaking, the combining sets the seeded human on the way to gradual physical AND mental unfoldment processes both innate and inherent.

In this sense, the human is as much prepackaged to unfold as is the tree, or whatever else is prepackaged to grow, spread out, expand, open up, and blossom.

And whatever is prepackaged to grow, expand, etc., is prepackaged with innate prepackaged powers to do so.

In this specific sense, unfoldment clearly applies to prepackaged powers that not only can, but also will unfold -- IF nurturing conditions are present for doing so.

This is then to wonder what the human would be like if the fuller spectrum of human prepackaged powers was nurtured and more fully unfolded.

Alas! As has been laboriously discussed throughout Volume I, human-designed societal power structures and contrived social conditioning systems have something to say about what is and is not to be nurtured.

The best way to ensure non-nurturing of something is simply to prevent awareness of it in the first place, either with regard to societal or individual contexts.

This is more specifically to state that if individuals can be made unaware of their innate unfoldment powers, then the chances are very good that most of them will mostly remain folded up and hence closed down and turned off -- i.e., NOT empowered.

This is a good juncture to wonder if individuals are aware not only of what their innate powers are, but if they are aware of the full spectrum of them?

There is no encyclopedia of human powers to help one identify anything along these. Because of the absence of this really important and much needed encyclopedia, one can remain unaware of one's innate powers.

One place to begin stimulating empowerment is simply to initiate awareness of the innate unfoldment powers -- thereby changing the ratio of aware/unaware equation regarding them. In this sense, initiating self-awareness of one's own innate powers is the single most self-central domain of the individual.

SUGGESTED EXERCISE

MAKE AN EFFORT TO LOCATE AND OBSERVE INSTANCES OF UNFOLDMENT IN HUMAN ACTIVITIES THESE INSTANCES CAN SOMETIMES BE IDENTIFIED WHERE ONE THING NATURALLY LEADS, IN SOME POSITIVE SENSE, TO ANOTHER, THEN TO ANOTHER, AND SO FORTH

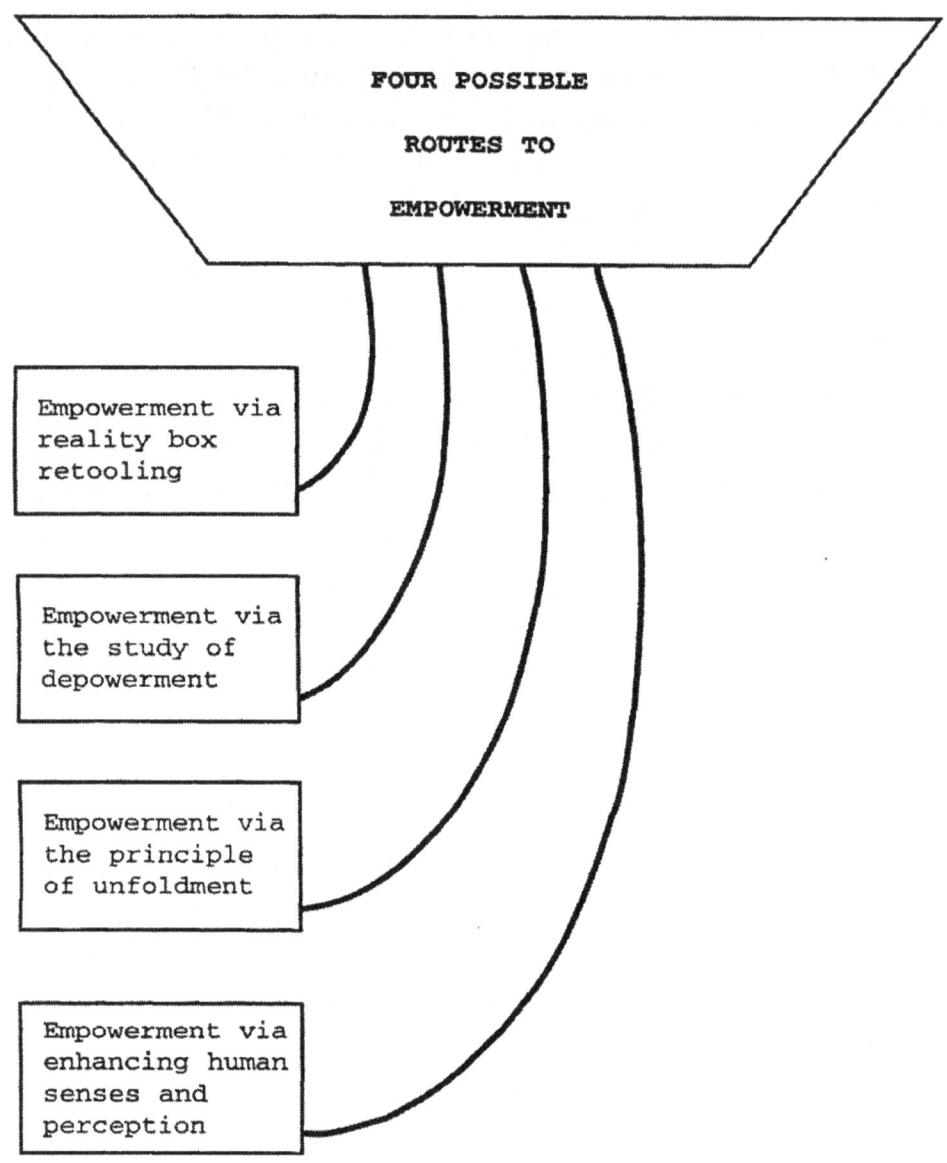

FIGURE 9. As a general rule of thumb, empowerment almost certainly requires increases in awareness in numerous directions, and so anything that increases this or that kind of it will in some sense turn out to be useful and vitalizing since all formats of awareness are interactive and recombinant.

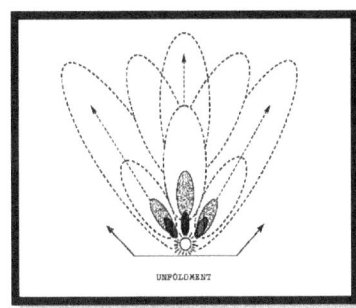

Chapter 19

EMPOWERMENT VIA ENHANCING HUMAN SENSES AND PERCEPTION

MOST WILL agree that if one cannot perceive or see something, then one doesn't have much of chance of gaining in power with respect to it.

To a lesser extent, it is also known that what is not perceived can have power over those who do not perceive it.

These two statements seem logical and innocent enough. However, between them are some subtle elements having rather serious implications with regard to empowerment.

Among the first of the subtle elements is the fact that most have little or no understanding of the dynamics of perception, how perception actually works, or what perception actually consists of.

This lack of understanding is NOT the fault of the individual.

The fault belongs to societal educational agendas mostly designed and set up during the modernist nineteenth and twentieth centuries. Those agendas taught that humans possessed only five physical senses of sight, smell, taste, touch, and hearing.

This teaching of the five physical senses was not so bad in itself -- because we do have those senses, and they do lead to perceptions of the physical.

But that teaching was accompanied by the related teaching that the human had NO OTHER senses.

THIS teaching was very bad. It has had tremendous negative consequences and has caused much needless suffering. Indeed, it has distorted almost all ideas of what the human actually is.

As it later turned out, senses additional to the five physical ones began to achieve rather grudging scientific recognition during the 1960s.

And as scientific developments advanced through the 1970s, these additional senses were ultimately surveyed in the book entitled DECIPHERING THE SENSES: THE EXPANDING WORLD OF HUMAN PERCEPTION, by Robert Rivlin and Karen Gravelle, published by Simon and Schuster in 1984.

As the authors put it, "For centuries we have used an oversimplified and inaccurate model to explain the human senses. Even now [i.e., in 1984], high school biology classes still teach 'the five senses.' But recent scientific research has discovered there are many more than five senses and has radically changed our understanding of what the senses are and how they work."

Indeed, no less than SEVENTEEN senses are reviewed in the book, and many more have been discovered since 1984.

However, knowledge of our multiple senses has not yet trickled down very actively into the masses of individuals who could benefit from that knowledge, especially those interested in empowerment and gaining in power.

Indeed, the 1984 book came -- and went -- with hardly any notice of it within societal mainstream educational agendas.

SENSE ORGANS VIS-À-VIS PERCEPTION

The term "senses" is one of those words utilized with what might be called sloppy dexterity -- in that we talk of "our senses" without at all realizing too much about them.

And so it is worthwhile taking a moment to remind that SENSE ORGANS constitute the basis for senses, in the absence of which we would not have senses to begin with.

The importance of sense organs will become more visible as this book proceeds.

In the biological sense, an ORGAN is defined as "a differentiated structure consisting of cells and tissues and performing some specific function; also, bodily parts performing a function or cooperating in an activity -- as, for example, eyes and related structures that make up the visual organs or ears and related structures that make up the hearing organs."

This is a delightful definition, especially when it becomes understood that if we don't have sense organs that receive and convey "information" of various kinds, then we will NOT have perceptions.

But there is a further important clue available here.

If we can think we have sense organs that specialize in various kinds of perceptions, some of which or a lot of which are not active and working, then we might comprehend that we will NOT have their specializing perceptions either.

To bring some further illumination upon this issue, one can merely ask if sense organs and their resulting senses can be dumbed down or "turned off."

One cannot usually see this in self, at least at first. But one can look around at others, which the student of empowerment must do for any number of valid reasons to be pointed up ahead.

A full part of this matter of sense organs is that while we realize we do sense this or that, we are unaware of the sense organs from which what we sense is coming. THIS, to be sure, is an important matter, as will be seen in chapter 21 ahead.

POWER RELATIVE TO PERCEPTIONS

One of the situations that can account for lack of the trickling-down of information about our MULTIPLE SENSES is that our senses and perceptions have hardly ever been discussed in the contexts of power and empowerment.

This is thus to say that PERCEPTIONS and POWER have never been discussed as adjacent and related to each other.

It stands to reason that more perceptions might equate to more empowerment -- while it is obvious that less perceptions can equate to larger proportions of depowerment.

For additional clarity here, it is worthwhile considering that each individual has a potential perception spectrum of 100 per cent.

Because of educational agendas and local environmental influences, most individuals utilize, say, only 10 percent or less of that spectrum.

Additionally, the chances are very good that the 10 percent refers only to the physical 3-dimensional universe -- and THEN only to smaller local versions of physicality that one has been mentally educated or programmed to grow up in and fit into.

If such is the situation, and if one can grok it, then achieving empowerment on any grand scale is somewhat doubtful.

In any event, as reviewed several times in Volume I, something like this constitutes the depowerment "trap" that is so valuable to the powerful few that control, relegate, and do not encourage wide-scale empowerment among the masses.

STANDARD DEFINITIONS OF PERCEPTION

Most trustworthy dictionaries provide TWO principal, but rather simplified, definitions of PERCEPTION:

1. Awareness of the elements of environment through physical sensation, and physical sensation interpreted in the light of experience;
2. Direct or intuitive cognition, insight, and a capacity for comprehension.

In the average dictionary, these two definitions are presented and compressed together with such ease that one might not at first notice the rather large and pregnant distinctions between them.

The distinctions come more into view if, for example, one considers perception as related to empowerment.

Perceptions derived from 3-dimensional physicality are always important, of course.

But with regard to empowerment and power, those kinds of perception characterized via the second definition are obviously more applicable.

Via the two contrasting definitions, it would be obvious that two highly different kinds, levels, sets, or spectrums of mind-like faculties are being described:

1. Perception faculties relevant to physicality;
2. Perception faculties relevant to what is NOT physical.

In passing here, it is worth noting that the English dictionary term PERCEPTION is derived from the Latin PERCEPTUS -- the principal meaning of which was something like the modern idea of CONSCIOUSNESS-OBSERVING. However, this definition, while noted, is given as "obsolete" for reasons that escape rational explanation.

It is also worth noting that only one synonym is given for perception -- discernment.

THE PERCEPTIBLE

That several different kinds of PERCEPTION exist is NOT made too clear if one consults the definitions for that term -- and each of which can act as "helpers" regarding empowerment processes.

However, we have a bit of better luck in consulting the definition for PERCEPTIBLE -- which is briskly identified as "capable of being perceived."

Two little facts can be deduced from this: (1) that humans can or might have perceptions of (2) what is capable of being perceived. One's mental equipment need not be all that profound in order to figure this out.

Six synonyms are given for PERCEPTIBLE, and with these the earnest student of empowerment hits some kind of subtle pay dirt. All of the synonyms refer to what is "apprehensible as real or existent." They are:

PERCEPTIBLE: applies to what can be discerned by the senses to the smallest extent.

SENSIBLE: applies to what is clearly though not markedly seen, heard, smelled, sometimes in contrast to what is discerned only by the intellect.

PALPABLE: applies either to what has physical substance or to what is obvious and unmistakable.

TANGIBLE: suggests what is capable of being handled or grasped both physically and mentally.

APPRECIABLE: applies to what is distinctly discernable by the senses or definitely measurable.

PONDERABLE: suggests having definitely measurable weight or importance, especially as distinguished from eluding such determination.

PERCEPTIVE – PERCEPTUAL

Two definitions are given for the term PERCEPTIVE:

1. Capable of or exhibiting keen perception;
2. Responding to sensory stimulus, characterized by sympathetic understanding or insight.

Both of these definitions are related to the concept of "observant" or "being observant."

Only one definition is given for the term PERCEPTUAL: "of, relating to, or involving sensory stimulus as opposed to abstract concept."

SUGGESTED EXERCISE

TAKE SOME CONVENIENT TIME AND MAKE A LIST OF THE SENSES YOU HAVE HOLD THIS LIST AND REVIEW IT AFTER READING THIS BOOK

PART FOUR
ALL INDIVIDUALS HAVE RECOGNIZABLE INNATE BASE POWER SYSTEMS

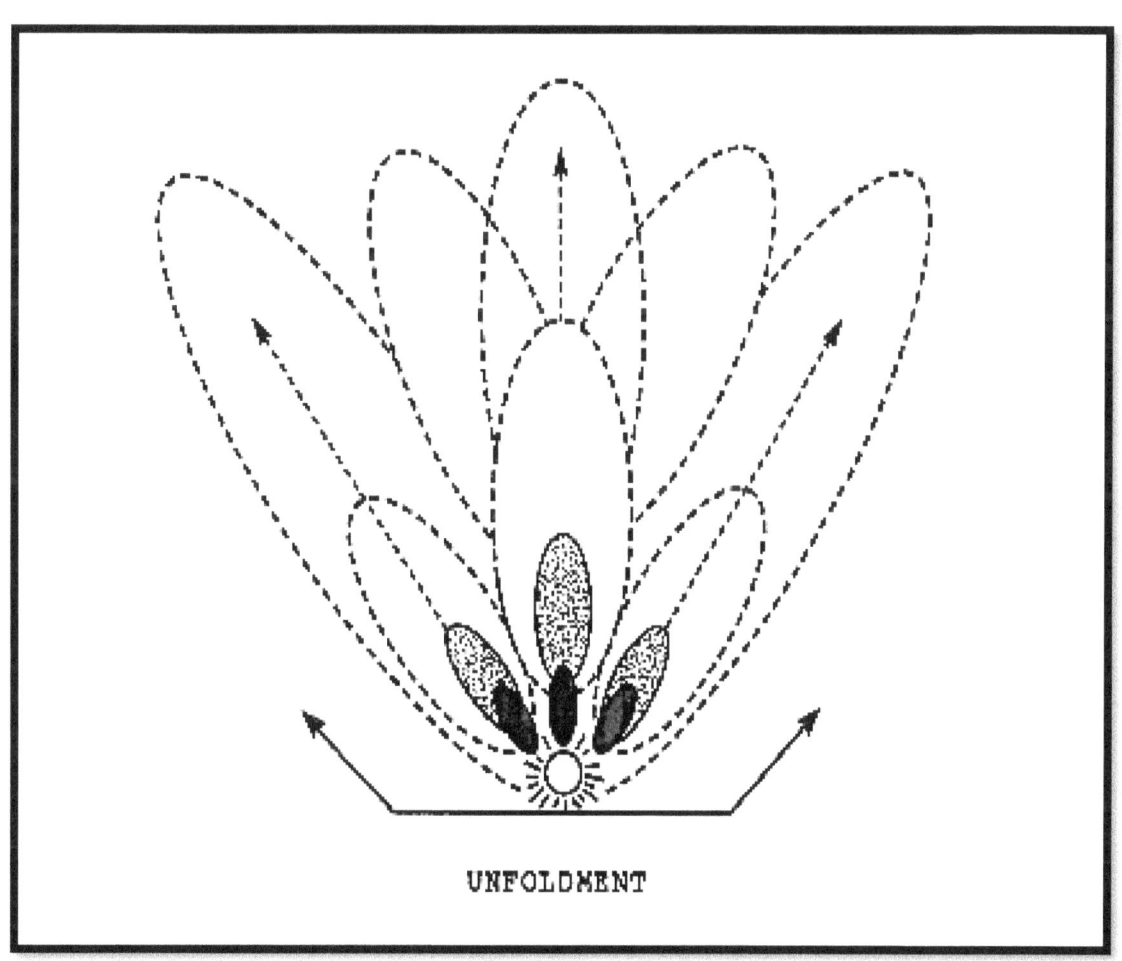

UNFOLDMENT

Chapter 20

THE REAL EXISTENCE OF POWER FACTORS

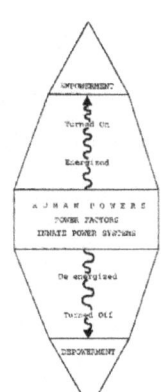

AS IS always worth repeating in these volumes, the absence of knowledge about empowerment has come about because of intrigues within various kinds of power structures that socially engineer two major classes of people -- the powerful and the powerless.

This traditional, on-going activity requires that the minds of individuals be socially shaped so as to especially result in powerless classes.

There are many ways of achieving this. By far the best historically proven way is simply to conceal the fact that all individuals are innately born with minds equipped with power systems.

When this fact is successfully concealed (via installed illiteracy and ignorance), the minds of individuals can be shaped or conditioned so as to fit the designs of this or that social power structure rather than to fit and accord with the extensive and amazing dimensions of the mind itself.

To emphasize: minds are shaped not in the light of their own remarkable dimensions and powers but are shaped to fit within the limits of artificial societal patterns.

Even during the modern period when the concept of establishing universal literacy gained in importance, information and knowledge about individual power and empowerment has remained almost totally absent or inaccessible.

In keeping with this artificial situation regarding powers of the individual it can be observed that many think that some individuals have them, but that most others do not.

In better actuality, it is the human species that has powers, and which innately download into each individual.

It is AFTER this downloading that the innate powers can be nurtured or not -- which is to say, turned on or turned off.

As an analogy here, it can be thought that each individual is born with something like a computer hard drive that is extensively pre-equipped with many powers.

Only some of these pre-equipped powers are needed to adapt to this or that social environment. In this sense, it is the social environments that provide the equivalent of software that can be programmed into the hard drive.

Needless to say, adapting to social environments usually demands the turning off of more powers than are turned on.

The processes involved with this are usually determined by the power structure inhabiting this or that social environment -- while the power structures themselves are set up and based on the idea that some few are to have power(s) while the larger majority are NOT to have them.

It is possible to examine societal power structures in detail, including their methods and techniques for gaining and maintaining control of the majority.

It turns out that the best method for achieving the control is to keep the intelligence powers of the majority as turned off as possible.

This is easily accomplished by ensuring that no knowledge packages about empowerment become visible.

If this method is relatively successful, then a so-called "average" level of intelligence among the many will not be too high -- but it will be okay to have that level because so many others likewise have it, and it therefore seems that is just the way things naturally are.

THE CONCEALMENT OF POWER FACTORS

Meanwhile, back at the greater ranch of our species itself, it is generally broadcast that possession of remarkable intelligence is its principal hallmark.

Yet, if power structures are examined, including those that have collapsed or self-destructed, it is often to be wondered how, or IF, intelligence has been conceptualized in them, including the presumed intelligence of the powerful.

In any event, the purpose of the foregoing discussion has been to bring to light that the existence of remarkable intelligence in our species, together with the social management of it in its individuals, is of fundamental, or base, importance with respect to ANY concept of empowerment.

The reason is obvious, once one can become aware of it. For if intelligence overall is not empowered or re-empowered, then it is entirely doubtful that empowerment can ultimately consist of little more than a laughing matter.

Of course, intelligence is rarely discussed in relationship to empowerment, largely because issues of empowerment are usually avoided altogether.

Indeed, this was certainly the case during the twentieth century, otherwise once referred to as the Age of Progress and as the Age of Psychology, during which the disciplines of psychology grew so much in importance as to require their own encyclopedias and dictionaries.

Yet, one can read through numerous dictionaries of psychological terms and not find the term EMPOWERMENT at all, and certainly not pointed up in connection to intelligence.

However, attention must herewith be drawn to a particular DICTIONARY OF PSYCHOLOGY compiled by J.P. Chaplin and published in 1968 by Dell Publishing Co.

The blurb on the back cover of this dictionary advertises that it "is the most recent compilation of terms, movements, and leading figures in the field of psychology, encompassing the many varieties and techniques that have evolved in the history of psychological thought."

For those who read dictionaries of such kinds, perchance to discover something important, this book is indeed a good and exciting read.

Even so, there is, of course, no entry in it for EMPOWERMENT, and the entry for POWER consists of the usual -- "muscular strength; ability or authority to control others; social power."

But there IS, of all things unusual, an entry for POWER FACTOR. And this is briskly defined as: "An intellectual factor which serves as an energizer of other intellectual factors."

While it is not indicated in the dictionary, this definition is most certainly one of the more significant definitions of empowerment, largely because it indicates a concept of energizing and relates it to intelligence.

It can be pointed out that the terms "intellectual" and "intelligence" do not mean exactly the same things, but the links between them are clear enough.

ENERGIZING OF POWER FACTORS

The meaning of ENERGIZER, however, IS clear enough, and, as has already been discussed, it is meaningful to both empowerment and depowerment -- for, at base, depowerment is merely the de-energizing of empowerment and of power factors.

There is no doubt that intelligence IS accepted as a human power, even if conventional attitudes do not view it as such.

What is seldom brought to light has to do with the identities of other base powers that need to be energized so as to energize, or re-energize, the power(s) of intelligence.

And, indeed, if other powers are dumbed down, or turned off, or remain innate but latent, then the threshold activity of base power intelligence will probably not be augmented (expanded, energized) all that much.

Thus, it is possible to arrive at a fundamental question having to do with whether intelligence is a separate thing-in-itself, or whether it is linked to, and even dependent upon, other base powers.

Many discussions, some of them quite dramatic, have taken place with regard to determining what intelligence IS.

But beyond THAT question, it is obvious that one of the basic functions of intelligence is to deal with information. So it is useful to wonder how intelligence gets information in the first place.

After all, if systems of intelligence are to deal with information, they first need to receive or acquire it. To help illuminate and grok this, we can now enter into a brief survey of one of the most astonishing discoveries of all times -- human information receptors at the cellular level of everyone.

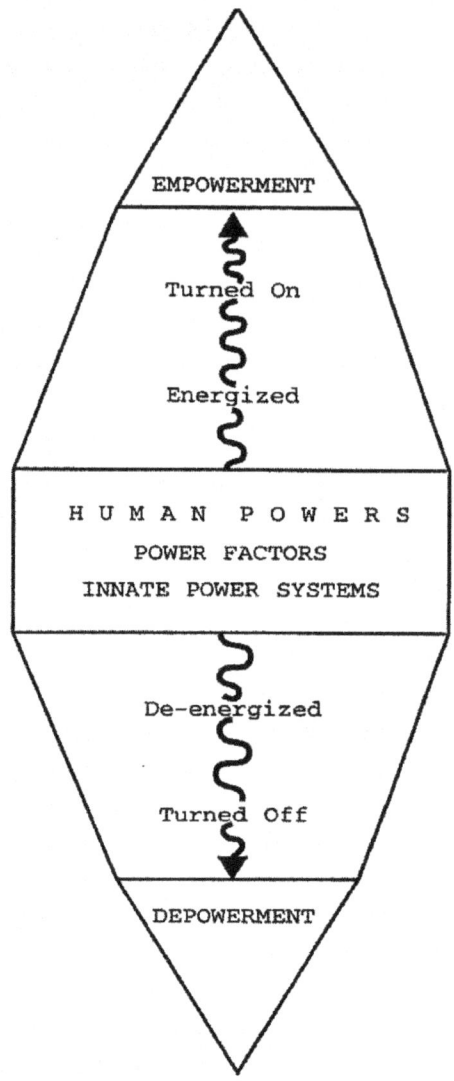

FIGURE 10. It is clear that social conditioning can energize or de-energize innate human powers in individuals, and this much is admitted by researchers of social conditioning processes. One of the results of this is that more human powers are turned off than are ever turned on. This, in turn, results in deficits and absences of information and knowledge about human powers in general, and so clear pictures of the real scope of human powers are generally unavailable. Thus, knowledge of the scope of human powers is also not present within individual reality boxes. Introduction of such knowledge can begin to re-energize numerous innate sensing systems that have been rendered inoperative via the limiting formats of social conditioning processes.

Chapter 21

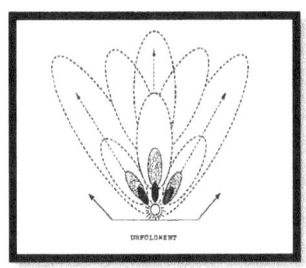

EACH HUMAN INDIVIDUAL IS EXTENSIVELY WIRED WITH INFORMATION RECEPTORS

THERE IS a general tendency to be concerned with WHAT information consists of, rather than with how the human organism in-takes information, gets it, or becomes aware of it, in the first place.

In other words, mind-intelligence must first in-take information before it can determine what it means one way or another. Thus, first there is in-take of information, and then there are the meanings to be assigned to various kinds and categories of it.

To repeat, if the human organism and its systems of powers of intelligence are to deal in and with information, there must first be ways and means of receiving it into the systems. Thus, if intelligence does not or cannot receive information, or various kinds of it, then it cannot deal with it.

The concern with what information consists of often leads to information management having to do with what people should or should not learn or acquire knowledge of, and this kind of thing is what social conditioning revolves around.

For example, information about empowerment can be made unavailable, and hence an absence of information about it can be artificially constructed.

In any event, if the human organism did not have ways and means of acquiring information, then its intelligence powers would have nothing to work with.

On the other hand, if intelligence receives only certain kinds of information, and does not receive other kinds, then it is probably somewhat trapped within the limits of the kinds it does have access to.

INFORMATION VIA THE 5-PHYSICAL SENSES

It is generally accepted that the human organism acquires information via the senses. As is well known, the modernist materialist concept of the sense organs held that there were only five of them -- and that the five-process sensory awareness of physicality. This concept was accepted as scientific doctrine.

As has been discussed, there was nothing wrong with this, as far as it went.

But the modernist concept also held that there were no other senses than the five physical ones, and therein a blunder of some magnitude became established as scientific "fact."

To a certain degree, the adherents of the doctrine can be forgiven their blunder, for they had no scientific way of ascertaining that additional sense organs existed.

But all along there were copious amounts of anecdotal evidence that humans also processed various kinds of sensed information that had little to do with physicality or the five physical senses.

Those kinds of sensed information were explained away as being merely "subjective" in nature, i.e., as interior products of mind, and which were not derived from any kind of physical sensing organs or systems.

THE DISCOVERY OF BIO-CELLULAR RECEPTORS

However, a great change regarding all of this began to occur when the first electron microscopes became available during the 1930s.

Examination of cells and cellular tissues under these microscopes began to reveal the existence of various kinds of RECEPTORS -- and this has culminated today in the understanding that every cell in the human organism (some trillions of them) does act as some kind of information-dealing receptor.

To understand this properly, is it fair to warn that the concepts and terminology of the old model of the five physical senses cannot continue to be used to any great benefit. Indeed, even the term "senses" cannot really be used with any great efficiency.

Instead, it is necessary to think not in terms of senses, but in terms of receptors and information.

And this shift in nomenclature also includes the physical five senses, which can more accurately be redefined as receptors of information confined exclusively to the limits of the receptors.

DEFINITIONS OF RECEPTORS

The term RECEPTOR is defined as: "a cell or group of cells acting as a sense organ that receive stimuli."

The word STIMULI (plural of STIMULUS) is defined as "something that arouses or incites to activity."

This is a slightly inefficient definition largely because the interdependent relationship between stimulus and receptor cannot easily be deduced from it.

In order to better grasp the fundamental nature of the relationship, the term ENERGETIC has to be considered.

That term is defined as "marked by energy" and "operating with vigor and effect."

And so the relationship between stimulus and receptor is an energetic one, in that the receptor is designed to energetically respond to this or that thing that stimulates the energetic response.

The term RECEPTOR was being used in English at about 1400, but generally meant someone who received something, while the term RECEIVER gradually replaced receptor in that particular usage.

The term RECEPTIVE was in use about 1547, and was defined as "having the quality, or capacity, for receiving; able to receive; pertaining to or of the nature of reception." This definition was in general usage from the seventeenth through the nineteenth centuries.

At about 1906, however, the term RECEPTOR began to be affiliated with certain biological structures having the capacity to receive energetic impulses of some kind -- i.e., receptor cells or cell groups, organs, and biodynamic systems.

By 1927, two concepts had been added to the 1906 definition of RECEPTORS:

"The receptor organs are those parts of the living organism which are specially sensitive to changes going on around them;" and

"To pick out and distinguish the different elements and qualities of which the world is composed, and which is made possible for higher animals by the enormous development of their receptor systems."

DISCOVERY OP RECEPTORS VIA ELECTRON MICROSCOPES

The first electron microscope was developed in Germany in 1932, and later evolved into more refined models in the United States and Canada.

With these remarkable instruments in hand, cellular biology underwent a great jump in importance -- and thus began the process of discovering that biological cells were not simplistic things as once thought.

Instead, they were composed of ultra-minute factors that functioned in amazing ways having to do not with physicochemical elements alone, but also with electromagnetic impulses.

The fact that biological organisms have some kind of electromagnetic substrate had been discovered during the seventeenth century. But this substrate was considered "weak" and thus unimportant in the face of the chemical substrate that was thought to be very strong.

During the 1930s, however, researchers in various parts of the world, and especially in the (now former) Soviet Union, began to realize that although the electromagnetic substrate was "weak," it nevertheless played very important roles within the bio-chemical whole of biological organisms.

In 1962, in Prance, a short paper by V. Mironovitch was published in REVUE

METAPSYCHIQUE. The paper reported on a number of discoveries and was entitled "The cells of the organism that act as receptors and emitters of electromagnetic waves," and reported on a number of discoveries.

Among these was the discovery that cells have activities that are akin to semi-conductors that "capture" electromagnetic waves and transform their energies into "a nervous flux" that then affects the physiological state of the organism.

In that sense, Mironovitch indicated that the cellular systems were acting in ways equivalent to "electromagnetic antennas," and that the cells not only received but also emitted and transmitted electromagnetic "signals" or impulses.

Mironovitch (and other French researchers) held that via its cellular "information" receptors "our organism is very intimately linked into all areas of ambient activity," including meteorological effects of the terrestrial atmosphere (such as pressure, temperature, humidity, and electrical charges), but also is directly exposed to and connected with cosmic radiations.

Based on this, and other discoveries, Mironovitch then suggested that the transmission of thought should indeed be possible because of, and via, biophysical receptors and emitters.

EXPANDED RECEPTOR RESEARCH

During the 1960s and 1970s, a tremendous amount of research about receptors began accumulating in scientific journals. It was not until 1984 that the importance of such work was published in a book format accessible to the lay reader. This book has been mentioned earlier, and, with emphasis, is again highly recommended to anyone seriously interested in empowerment.

As already referred to, it is entitled DECIPHERING THE SENSES: THE EXPANDING WORLD OF HUMAN PERCEPTION, jointly authored by Robert Rivlan and Karen Gravelle, published by Simon & Schuster (1984). To quote from the book's flyleaf:

"For centuries we have used an oversimplified and inaccurate model to explain the human senses. Even now, high school biology classes still teach the 'five senses'. But recent scientific research has discovered that there are many more than five senses, and these discoveries have radically changed our understanding of what the senses are and how they work. [The authors] redefine for the general reader the spectrum of human perceptions from the normal to the newly discovered to the extra-sensory."

SOME DIFFERENT TYPES OF HUMAN RECEPTORS THAT HAVE BEEN DISCOVERED

The following is a partial list of human receptors that are now known to exist.

Please bear in mind that although the receptors are considered to be minute physical "organs" dealing in some kind of sensing, what they do "sense" constitutes some kind of impulse-like "information."

1. Receptors in the nose sensing system that smell emotions, and that can identify motives, sexual receptivity, antagonism, benevolence, etc.
2. Receptors in the ear sensing systems that detect and identify differences in air pressure and electromagnetic frequencies.
3. Skin receptors that detect balance and imbalance regarding what is external to the bio-body, even external at some astonishing distances.
4. Skin receptors that detect motion outside of the body, even when the body is asleep.
5. Directional finding and locating receptors in the endocrine and neuropeptide systems.
6. Whole-body receptors, including hair, that identify fluidic motions of horizontal, vertical, diagonal, even if not visually perceived.
7. Skin receptors that "recognize" the temperament of other biological organisms.
8. Subliminal sensory systems that locate and identify pitch of sound, a sense of heat across great distances, a sense of frequencies and waves, either mechanical or energetic.
9. Receptors that identify positive and negative charged particles at the atomic level.
10. Microsystems transducing of various forms of mechanical, chemical, and electromagnetic energy into meaningful nerve impulses -- i.e., into information.
11. Receptors that sense gravitational changes.
12. Neurological receptors for interpreting modulated electronic information by converting it into analog signals for mental storage.
13. Bioelectric receptors for sensing radiation, including X-rays, cosmic rays, infrared radiation, and ultraviolet light, all of these receptors being found in the retina of the eye.
14. Receptors that respond to exterior electrical fields and systems.
15. Skin receptors for sensing perceptions of bonding or antagonism.
16. Senses for non-verbal "language" communicating.

17. Combined sensing systems (neural networks) for making meaning out of at least 130 identified non-verbal physical gestures and twenty basic kinds of non-verbal messages.
18. Receptors that trigger alarm and apprehension before their sources are directly perceived consciously.
19. Sensing systems for registering and identifying non-verbal emotional waves.
20. Receptors in the pineal gland that sense and store memory of light and darkness, anticipating them with accuracy as the daily motions of the sun and moon change.
21. Receptors in the pineal gland that sense solar and lunar rhythms, solar disruptions (flares, sunspots) and moon-caused tidal changes, coming earthquakes and storms.
22. If the pineal gland is fully functional, it acts as a non-visual photoreceptor, the psychic equivalent being "X-ray vision."
23. Whole-body receptors (millions of them) to detect pheromones, sexual attitudes, fear, love, admiration, danger, pain in others, intentions in others, etc.

RECEPTORS (AND EMITTERS) AS POWERS OF MIND AND INTELLIGENCE

As the cutting edge of research into receptors has progressed, it is now generally understood that all life forms possess some kind of them, and it is understood that they are innate within the species genomes of life forms and are thus downloaded into each individual of the species.

Although this might come as a surprise to most, all human individuals are thus innately equipped with the receptors described in the twenty-three categories above.

What has not yet clearly been brought into the light of understanding about receptors, however, is that they can be referred to as powers -- in that they deal in energy reception and modulate and/or transform it into meaning and "information" of various kinds that can be recognized as such by appropriate neural network systems.

The number of receptor-emitters within human cellular-neural systems is vast enough to be thought of as astronomical -- and the direct implication is that they altogether constitute energy-dynamic substrates of mind-cum-intelligence.

What is also not yet fully recognized about receptor research is that it will, in the nearing future, ultimately change how the human organism is thought of. And when receptor research is coupled with genome research, ways and means will doubtlessly be found to genetically enhance receptor-emitter activity.

EXPERIENCING RECEPTOR-EMITTER ACTIVITY AT THE INDIVIDUAL LEVEL

Whether they realize it or not, many individuals do experience sensing phenomena that download from basic receptor-emitter activity, and some reading through the foregoing list of the twenty-three kinds might by now have recognized as much.

Various sensing systems based in this or that receptor activity can even be enhanced by increasing awareness of them, and this kind of thing is especially found in several of the martial arts, and especially that of Aikido in which increases of general awareness at the autonomic levels are actually tutored.

Those reading through the list of twenty-three above will also recognize the receptor-emitter basis for various types of intuition and other kinds of ultra-sensing that extend beyond the boundaries of the famous 5-physioal senses.

Indeed, while the concept of cellular receptors might be relatively new, many of their phenomena are actually quite familiar.

THE DYNAMIC STATUS OF RECEPTOR RESEARCH AS REFLECTED IN THE INTERNET

In the publishing and media industries, reports on the cutting edges of receptor research are few and far between.

But as most have begun to realize, the search engines in the Internet have become fountains of all kinds of information. So it is to the Internet search engines that readers interested in receptors are directed.

For example, as of the middle of 2001, the GOOGLE search engine lists well over one-half million references about receptors. Especially relevant are those references pointing to the categories of science, biology, cell biology, signal transduction, and etc.

The bottom line here is that each individual has trillions of receptors -- but this factor has never before been integrated into past models of mind, intelligence, or empowerment.

Individuals therefore have innate powers with respect to whatever their receptors have powers for.

SUGGESTED EXERCISE

ONE CAN READ THROUGH THE LIST OF RECEPTORS ABOVE AND MAKE NOTES OF WHATEVER IN ONE'S EXPERIENCE SEEMS SUGGESTIVE OR FAMILIAR

Chapter 22

EVERYONE HAS AT LEAST TWO INNATE SENSING SYSTEMS

SENSED INFORMATION UPLOADS THROUGH LENSES OF AWARENESS

THE MANY discoveries having to do with receptors establish that the human organism is extensively wired for participating within exchanges of information at all levels of mind, including whatever its different parts might consist of.

This needs to be put even more descriptively. Each individual is genetically receptor-wired in a hard drive kind of way.

Each, therefore, has an enormous range of information receptors that are innately present in the same way that the skeleton, muscles, organs, and neural systems are present.

Thus, because of the discoveries regarding receptors, it is possible to conceptualize each individual not only as a physical body, but also as a very elaborate array of information sensing systems living amid a universe of information in the form of waves, signals, energies, and impulses.

Something like this has, in fact, been understood here and there in the past, and in various ways. For example, it has long been understood that some life forms simply respond to their environments.

Other life forms, however, intervene in their environments, and do so via a lesser or greater modicum of that factor called "intelligence:" for example, termites, bees, beavers, weaver birds, and, of course, humans who generally hold themselves to be the top-of-the-line regarding intelligence.

Thus have arisen accepted distinctions between lower "stimulus-response" life organisms, and those higher life organisms somehow having possession of information-dealing formats of intelligence that can transcend the obvious limits of stimulus-response mechanisms.

One distinction between bio-stimulus-response organisms and those possessing intelligence is that the former responds only to what is immediately affecting them physically in some direct tangible sense.

However, those organisms possessing more or less greater modicums of intelligence not only can extend awareness into past, present, and. future contexts, but can also have awareness of tangible and intangible information.

Intangible information is derived from making deductions about what exists and detecting implications with or without tangible evidence for them.

Indeed, here is one of the major definitions of intelligence.

But this also means that higher forms of intelligence, such as those of humans, must actually possess two receptor sensing systems for dealing in two different kinds of information -- i.e., information tangible, and information intangible.

DIFFICULTIES IN IDENTIFYING THE TWO TYPES OF RECEPTOR SENSING SYSTEMS

Generally speaking, the term PERCEPTION is utilized to inclusively identify a multitude of phenomena. Some of those phenomena are different enough from others and should therefore be singled out and specified under some other nomenclature.

The problem here begins with standard dictionary definitions for PERCEPTION:

1. Consciousness (today given as obsolete.)
2. A result of perceiving; observation.
3. A mental image; a mental concept.
4. Awareness of elements of environment through physical sensation.
5. Physical sensation interpreted in the light of experience.
6. Direct intuitive cognition; insight.
7. A capacity for comprehension.

If these definitions are meditated upon, it can gradually dawn that they refer to a large variety of phenomena, the processes of which obviously do not derive from one source.

For example, there are great distinctions between "intuition-insight" and "awareness of the elements of environment through physical sensations" -- the greatest distinction being that the two categories are not the same at all.

However, the two categories ARE incorporated under the same word -- and one of the really dreadful results of this is that one is led to think that intuitive information is obtained the same way as information about the environment through physical sensations.

Since the differences between the two categories are so great, the processes behind each must be quite different.

It is thus that the definitions for perception, if somewhat helpful, are otherwise something of a snarl, and so it might be that the single term PERCEPTION should not be utilized in such a generalizing way.

GETTING BEYOND THE CONCEPT OF PERCEPTION

The increasing discovery regarding receptors of all kinds has, of course, put an end to the 5-senses only idea, although that idea still lingers on.

Even so, the five senses ARE powers innately present in each human individual, the principal function of which is to provide to the mind information about the physicality that is immediately surrounding each of them.

But human individuals do not operate-function exclusively within or because of physical-sensory surroundings, and it is easy enough to establish that they operate-function within information contexts that are NOT available from or because of physicality alone.

This clearly establishes that human individuals have powers in addition to those associated with physicality.

To get somewhat deeper into this, it is useful to review the history of the term PERCEPTION, if only to get beyond its boundaries.

The term PERCEPTION entered English at about 1493. It was taken from the Latin PERS1PERE, which, in its literal sense, meant "to take in, to receive." But the first English definition of PERCEPTION was "to take in rents."

By about 1611, the idea of "to take in cognizance of" began to be associated with PERCEPTION, and this gradually flowered into the metaphorical idea of "The taking cognizance or being aware of objects in general -- especially as distinct from volition."

In other words, becoming aware of objects in general was thought of as some kind of passive process, as distinguished from volition as an active one. And in fact, down until today, the perceptions of the five physical senses have essentially been thought of as PASSIVE intakes of information about physicality.

It was not until about 1827 and shortly thereafter that the definition of PERCEPTION was extended to include "the intuitive or direct recognition of a moral or aesthetic quality, e.g., the truth of a remark, the beautiful in objects."

The meaning implicit in this definition, however, refers to some kind of discriminating activity that is not exclusively based on the passive cognizance of objects as earlier defined.

Indeed, objects of and in themselves do not automatically reflect moral or aesthetic qualities that are passively recognized.

Such recognitions, if they are to exist and to arise in individuals, must be actively provided by other powers of mind whose functions are involved with deducing, with becoming cognizant of, and with recognizing QUALITIES.

Because of the cognitive difficulties involved with all of the above, a suggestive example is useful. Almost everyone can passively perceive the physical existence of rocks, and let it go at that.

It can, however, be deduced that rocks have many qualities of being useful: they can be used as weapons, for building walls and highways, and if the quality of beauty is added in, they can be compiled into wonderful and soaring architecture.

So a rock is not JUST a rock passively perceived via the passive information intakes of the physical senses,

The passive perception of rocks alone does not imply intelligence in the beholder. But subsequent management of their qualities is a testament to the presence of active powers of intelligence that are quite different from the passive powers of physical perception.

HUMAN POWERS PASSIVE AND ACTIVE

While this little discussion is probably somewhat painful, the point of it has been to introduce the very important distinctions between passive and active human powers, a distinction that is made difficult by incorporating both sets of powers under just one word: perception.

In fact, at about 1837, the existence of this difficulty began to be recognized by some researchers and philosophers seeking more intimately to sort out the confusions involved.

An attempt was therefore made to introduce the term PERCEPT -- and which was introduced as referring to (1) "the mental product or result of perceiving," and (2) "the object of perception."

The intention of these definitions is not at first crystal clear. The objects of perception, rocks for example, were, as objects, to be referred to as percepts -- while, at the same time the objects as percepts were to be duplicated within the human mind and thus to also be referred to as percepts.

So, both object-percept and mental-percept of it were percepts -- with the stipulation that the object outside of the perceiver evokes the mental-percept of it.

If one is slightly confused by now, not to worry. The attempt here was to indicate that objects and mental images of them were both percepts -- having to do with OBJECTS defined as physically existing.

The percept, as well as the idea of perception, was exclusively related to physicality. And while the term PERCEPT is not generally used, it can be found in most twentieth century dictionaries with the definition of: "An impression of an object [physical] obtained by the use of the [physical] senses."

Otherwise, the percept attempt was undertaken especially to begin recognizing the distinctions between direct perception of physical objects AND the becoming aware of mental activity that does not originate within the exact contexts of physical perception.

TANGIBLE AND INTANGIBLE INFORMATION

At the heart of this convoluted matter resides the simple distinction between kinds of information derived from physicality and kinds of information derived from other than physicality.

The human species is very good at deriving both kinds of information, the distinctions involving the differences not only between physical and non-physical, but between the seen and unseen, between the tangible and intangible, between the visible and invisible.

Because of advancing receptor research, one observation that it is now appropriate to make is that if human organisms did not have receptors having to do with nonphysical, unseen, intangible, invisible information, then such would not be available to any human organism. In other words, humans would not experience anything akin to intuition, or even insight or foresight.

It is thus possible to identify the real existence of TWO receptor systems having to do with the distinctions between the two categories.

One of the characteristics of intuition, insight, or foresight is that their products are mental products NOT derived exclusively from physicality, but rather via mixes of deduction and some kind of detecting that has not been very seriously identified.

Another of the characteristics is that instances of intuition, insight, and foresight can spontaneously occur in just about everyone -- meaning that deduction-detecting systems naturally exist even though there is general nonawareness of them.

It is also obvious that if intuition, and etc., yields, as it often does, information ultimately demonstrated as valid and applicable, then the real existence of detector systems in companionship with preceptor systems becomes recognizable.

HUMAN RECEPTOR INFORMATION SYSTEMS

PERCEPTOR SYSTEMS ⟷ DETECTOR SYSTEMS

Identify & Process — Identify & Process

Tangible, physical information — Intangible, non-information

SUGGESTED EXERCISE

MAKE QUIET ATTEMPTS TO OBSERVE OTHERS (1) WHO MERELY PERCEIVE THINGS and (2) THOSE WHO DETECT IMPLICATIONS AND HIDDEN MEANINGS

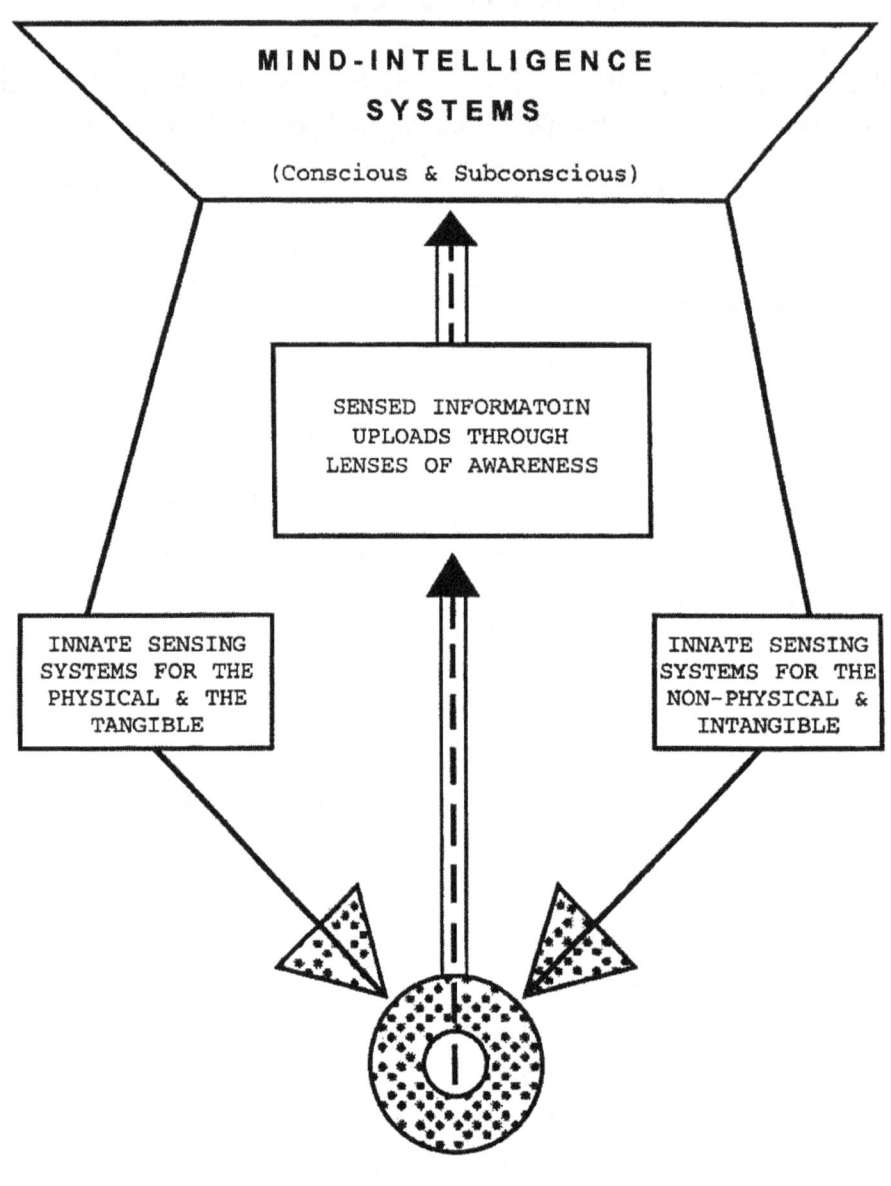

FIGURE 11. Tangible and intangible types of sensed information are probably filtered through lenses of awareness, and which, in turn, are probably shaped and/or depowered by constituents of different kinds of reality boxes. But the "equipment" for uploading both tangible and intangible information is innate in all individuals, regardless of whether the equipment is active or inactive.

Chapter 23

THE "ELECTRO-IMPULSE" BASIS OF PERCEPTOR AND DETECTOR INFORMATION SYSTEMS

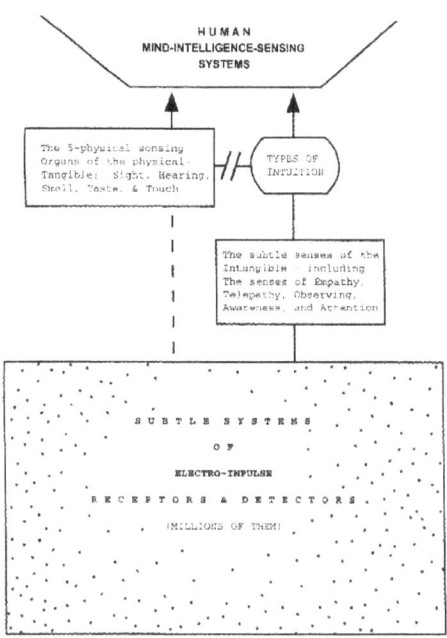

SCIENTIFIC ADVANCES have established that whatever else life forms might consist of, down at the cellular and molecular levels, they are electro-chemical-energetic in nature, and that if the electro parts go missing, the chemical and energetic parts begin failure closedown.

However, what the electro parts altogether consist of is not completely understood, except that some parts are electromagnetic (EM) in nature, while other parts follow some other undiscovered kinds of energetic principles.

To help provide a cognitive basis for this, the science of BIO-ELECTROCHEMISTRY deals with the relation of bioelectricity to bio-chemical changes and with the inter-conversion of biological chemical and electrical energy.

The term IMPULSE has several definitions. The principal one is given as "a wave of excitation transmitted through tissue and especially nerve fibers and muscles that results in physiological and mind-brain activity or inhibition of it."

The term INFORMATION also has several definitions. One of them, most unfamiliar, is given as "a signal impressed upon the input [or intake] of a communication system."

In connection with impulse and information, the term SIGNAL has two definitions: "Something that incites to action;" and "A detectable physical [or non-physical] quantity or impulse (as a voltage, current, or magnetic field strength) by which messages or information can be transmitted."

Thus, generally speaking, and in accordance with the foregoing definitions found in most dictionaries, impulses equal information, or at least some kind of it, while information equals different kinds of impulses that act as signals impressed upon the input or intake of receptor, preceptor, and detector sensing systems.

At this point, it is now useful to refer back to chapter 21 containing a list of some twenty-three human receptor-perceptor-detector systems that have been discovered in recent times, and which are innate, even if depowered or non-functioning, in all individual specimens of our human species.

However, the descriptions of the electronic receptors and impulses, and impulse information transmission via them, are quite alien to the conventional social conditioned ideas of what the individual human is -- a biological package only of bones, meat, appetites, nerves, having perhaps a mind or part of one, and which mind generally demonstrates only some lower level of intelligence activity.

In any event, since various distinctions have been made so far in this Part Four, it can now be wondered what information basically consists of, especially with respect to detection of information intangible.

THE "IMPULSE" BASIS OF INFORMATION

Concepts of what information basically consists of will doubtlessly undergo refinement in the future, especially regarding the enormous minute realms and levels of receptors.

But it can roughly be stated that information begins with impulses, or at least with some energetic factors that stimulate various kinds of receptors.

It can also be stipulated that information impulses must somewhere and somehow be "sensed-felt" within receptor sensing systems.

If they are, then, although information may exist and be available, it will not "enter" into impulse receptor system networks, or, for that matter, into mind-intelligence awareness systems.

It can easily be seen that information and empowerment have something to do with each other.

It can also be seen that if information AND its implications are not sensed-felt within individual mind-intelligence power systems, then whatever the information might consist of will remain absent in those systems.

And THIS is the principal reason for dragging through the following considerations about impulses and the two basic sensing systems innate in everyone.

THE MEANING OF INFORMATION IMPULSES TO EMPOWERMENT AND POWER

While certain definitions for the word IMPULSE have been mentioned above, there are additional ones to be pointed out:

1. The act of driving onward with sudden force;
2. A wave of excitation transmitted through the tissues and, especially, nerve fibers and brain synapses;
3. A force communicated or transmitted so as to produce motion suddenly with respect to incentive, inspiration, or motivation.

Combined, these three definitions of IMPULSE can just as well be taken, with some surprise, as one of the MOST IMPORTANT definitions of power. The definitions are relevant within the individual human organism and are also entirely relevant to larger-picture formats of power external to that organism.

Indeed, IMPULSE equals electrical/magnetic/power, which in turn equates to MEANING/INFORMATION, and which in turn again equates to some quantum of POWER and EMPOWERMENT.

Via the observations above, it can now be seen that electro-information impulses have some vital relevance to the status of power and empowerment not only regarding a given individual, but also with respect to "sources" of power external to individuals.

This is much to say that where there are few or no impulses, there will also not be much power. So to speak, the "action" is where the impulses are, or vice versa.

The foregoing discussions clearly imply that the individual, in addition to viewing self as a physical body with mental equipment, also needs to view self as composed of equipment that deals in and with electro-magnetic impulses.

Indeed, the individual organism could not experience impulses if the necessary equipment for doing so did not exist.

And so, one begins to wonder what that equipment might consist of.

It is logical to assume that the equipment, to work at all, must contain two fundamental factors that permit the intake and output of impulses -- or "signals."

As has been discussed, these two factors are referred to as biological receptors and emitters of electrical or magnetic impulses -- and which, for a long time, were held not to exist.

But the real existence of receptors and emitters has, by now, abundantly been confirmed scientifically -- although their overwhelming importance to human awareness has not yet trickled down too much as of this year, 2002.

While the matter of receptors and emitters may be unfamiliar, almost everyone can realize that specimens of our human species possess sensing systems, and so we are back on familiar territory.

It would be quite obvious, therefore, that receptors and emitters of impulses are the working parts of sensing systems, and which, indeed, could not work without intake and output of impulse signals.

If one begins to think in terms of human sensing systems, one might also begin to wonder if there is just one, or several, each of which somehow functions with respect to different kinds of information impulses.

SENSING SYSTEMS IMPULSES ARE TRANSDUCED INTO COGNIZABLE INFORMATION

It is admittedly difficult to conceptualize what an energy impulse actually consists of, especially because the impulses take place at a cellular level -- and so they are not exactly consciously experienced as such.

One way to get around this is to utilize the analogy of a radarscope on which blips appear when something they are engineered to contact comes into view.

But the blips ultimately need to be identified as to what they represent or mean -- and so some sort of process has to exist to convert the blip into something recognizable.

This process is, in some sense at least, a process akin to TRANSDUCTION.

A TRANSDUCER is defined as "a device that is actuated by power from one system and supplies power in any other form to a second system." The usual example given of a transducer is the telephone whose receiver is actuated by electric power and supplies acoustic power to the surrounding air.

In other words, the electric power is transduced into acoustic power.

With respect to human sensing systems that are actuated by impulses, the impulses need to be forwarded to some kind of transducing systems that convert the impulses into feeling and meaning that can become cognizable and recognizable to mind-intelligence, or to any other relevant mind-part -- such as the subconscious part.

Otherwise, if the transducing systems did not exist, the impulse signals would merely constitute mishmashes of unidentifiable noise, or not register at all in any system.

If THIS is difficult to understand, do be assured that no one so far knows anything about the details of human transducing systems except that the jump of converting impulse into feeling and meaning does take place.

As far as conscious experience might be concerned, there seem to be at least five transducing systems that convert impulses into feelings and meanings -- although before this book, these five have never been conceptualized as transducing systems.

But all five are known to exist, and all five are generally familiar enough, and if properly understood they can have ultra-importance with respect to empowerment. All of the five act as stimulating and energizing power factors to each other.

Alas, the five share one thing in common: in-depth information and knowledge about them is almost totally unavailable, and what little information does exist is encapsulated in confusions.

These five human transducing systems qualify as base powers pure and simple, and so they can be empowered or depowered -- which is to say, turned on or turned off.

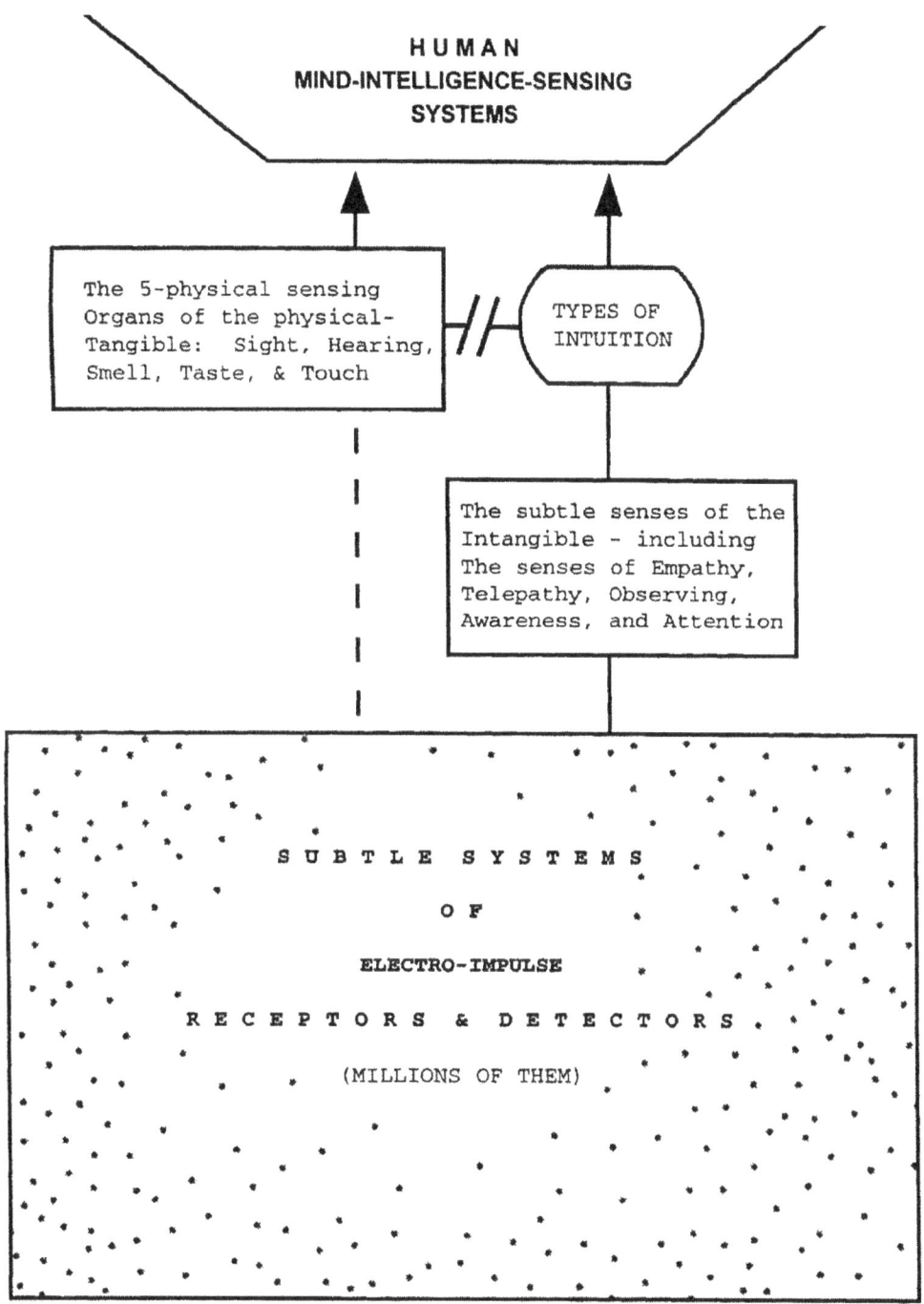

FIGURE 12. The 5-physical senses only concept forbids the existence of intuition, empathy, and telepathy, and so forth, and severely limits concepts of aware powers so as to include awareness of the physical only.

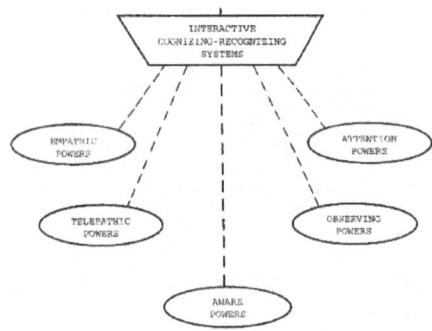

Chapter 24

HUMAN POWERS EMPATHIC

THOSE WHO examine the list of human receptors found in chapter 21 might begin to recognize some sensing phenomena they have experienced themselves or have surely read about.

Indeed, what can be called extended or exceptional senses are often featured in science fiction, in parapsychological literature, in anthropological studies of diverse kinds of cultures, and, of course, in movies that incorporate motifs of extraordinary human powers and performance.

As already discussed, the 5-senses-only idea could not explain why or how such phenomena could occur in anyone.

The advent of receptor research has provided the new reality that the human organism IS equipped, via its receptor systems, to participate in very many different kinds of sensing.

And so, for emphasis, it is the advent of receptor research that is providing new awareness of and fresh insight into any number of human powers.

It is, however, necessary to comprehend that the 5-physical senses and the receptor sensing systems DO NOT sense things in themselves, but sense pulse-like information about them.

Once sensed, this pulse-like information is forwarded into other mind systems that integrate it with memory, experience, understanding, and with whatever knowledge has accumulated.

Whether or not the integrations enter into the so-called conscious part of the mind is another matter.

The reason is that if the integrated information is to enter into that conscious part, it also has to enter into the reality boxes that characterize that part.

The chief characteristic of reality boxes is that they are structured upon specific and often quite limited frames of reference, and this condition might limit cognitive awareness at the conscious level.

Even so, it must be stipulated that receptor information IS entering the systems of the human organism. If it is not being accepted into the conscious part of mind, it is anyway being fed into other non-conscious parts of it where it can merge with subconscious activity.

After this, the receptor information can spontaneously emerge, for example, via dream states, intuition states, gut-feelings, foreseeing phenomena, and also affect emotional and empathic levels.

One of the great, but unacknowledged, powers of our species that downloads into everyone is the power to erect cognitive reality boxes whether based on lesser or greater amounts of emotional and intellectualized information.

It thus follows that one of the great tools of depowerment is to limit cognitive awareness of the amounts of information.

This, in fact, is easy enough to determine, for if individuals are kept in deprived information conditions, then they usually develop relatively powerless reality boxes.

It is quite clear that depowerment can be socially engineered by depriving reality boxes of information -- especially with respect to knowledge about power and empowerment.

As it must be, then, the adding of information to reality boxes equates to various kinds of empowerment, or at least begins the reverse of depowerment. For it is the conscious addition of information that can permit increased integration of larger amounts of information derived from the receptor sensing levels.

THE INTERACTIVE NATURE OF OUR OBSERVING, EMPATHIC, AND "TELEPATHIC" POWERS

On the list of receptor categories provided in chapter 21, attention is now drawn to item 23, which reads:

"Whole-body receptors (millions of them) to detect pheromones, sexual receptivity, fear, love, admiration, danger, pain in others, intentions in others, etc."

Bearing in mind these whole-body receptors, it is commonly understood that we do have five physical sensing powers.

The function of these is to sense impulse-elements of physicality and input what is sensed into the larger whole of conscious and non-conscious human awareness systems.

What is sensed, and input can be thought of as "information."

After the input, however, something must be done with or about the information, especially with regard to establishing the meaning(s) of the input information.

If no meanings are established, then the input information has zero importance, and the chances are very good that whatever has zero importance will not even format into perception or detection of it. This clearly and unambiguously means that human sensing systems not only have receptors that input "raw" information but MUST also have receptors that deal with attributing meaning(s) of what has been input as raw information.

THIS, in turn, clearly implies the existence of TWO essential systems -- one that inputs information-impulses, and one that assigns meaning to what has been input.

In order to help clarify that this double system does exist in actuality, the physical mechanisms of eyesight, for example, have been discovered and mapped down to and including their smallest biological molecules.

This has constituted a majestic effort, but at its end it is still not known how the physical mechanisms end up producing non-physical images in the brain-mind, or how meaning is attributed to what has been perceived.

One of the deterrents to discovery in this regard is that our human species possesses perceiving and detecting powers that are not, in their first instances, based on physicality.

And indeed, anyone who studies powers in some depth soon realizes that basic sets of non-physical powers do exist.

One such set is characterized by our empathic powers that "detect pheromones, sexual receptivity, fear, love, admiration, danger, pain in others, intentions in others, etc."

All of these are not so much tangible physical things as they are intangible qualities that must be deduced out of raw information input by basic receptors.

The English language has only one term that seems efficient here, the term EMPATHY.

THE TERM "EMPATHY"

It is now necessary to bring to light the definitions of certain terms which, when associated and combined into a knowledge package, will lead to realizations about how utterly important our empathic powers are.

It seems that the term EMPATHY was first brought into usage only in 1912 by a German writer named Lipps, and then only in association with art and art appreciation.

Lipps propounded the theory that the appreciation of a work of art depends upon the capacity of the spectator to project his personality into the object of contemplation. One had to "feel oneself into it."

In German, Lipps referred to this mental process as EINFUHLUNG, which was translated into English as EMPATHY.

Literally speaking, EM means "to put into" something.

The English term PATHETIC is taken from the Greek PATHETIKOS, meaning "capable of feeling."

EMPATHY thus means "to put into feeling."

However, to be precise, the German word EINFUHLLEN is defined as "to feel one's way into; to seek or obtain a sympathetic understanding."

Although SYMPATHETIC is usually thought of as having compassion and sensitivity to the emotions or situations of others, the principal definition is given as "existing or operating through an affinity, interdependence, or mutual association."

In 1928, the term EMPATHY was given another distinction, again with regard to art and art appreciation: "the active power of empathy which makes the artist, or as the passive power of empathy which makes the appreciator of art."

These are distinctions might be lost in today's status-conscious cultures in which "art" is defined by how much it costs, or what it will sell for at auction.

But in any event, the early definitions of empathy give some idea that it is probably a non-physical function of mind.

As it was by the 1930s, the definitions for EMPATHY were lifted out of their singular artistic associations and three additional ones were given as:

1. The power of entering into the experience or understanding of objects or emotions outside ourselves.
2. The capacity for participating in another's feelings or ideas.
3. The imaginative projection of a subjective state into an objective one so that the objects appears to be infused with it.

As discussed so far, it might seem that the idea of empathy is a relatively modern, and somewhat intellectual development.

But the idea of EMPATHY has some serious historical roots in that it is built upon the ancient Greek concepts of the PATHOS and the PATHETIC.

One of the difficulties with the term PATHETIC is that it has a modern definition and an ancient one, the latter of which is given as "obsolete."

The modern use: Affecting the tender emotions; exciting a feeling of pity, sympathy, or sadness.

The ancient use: Producing an effect upon the emotions; exciting the passions or affections; moving, stirring, affecting. (This definition, allegedly obsolete, is certainly not so in Hollywood, etc.)

TO FEEL is closely associated with physical touch, or to ascertain by physical touch. In a wider sense, it is also defined as:

1. To have the sensation of contact with;
2. To perceive, or be affected with sensation through those senses (receptors) which are not referred to any special organ, but through the condition of any part of the body (i.e., whole-body receptors);
3. To perceive (or detect) mentally, to become aware of.

The third definition above is indicated as obsolete, for reasons not entirely clear -- except, possibly, to intellectually sever the connection between empathic powers and powers of awareness.

To have the sensation of contact with, thence to put into feeling so as to become aware of, thence to perceive or detect mentally, can altogether be thought of as the processes of empathy.

The whole of these processes begins with impulse inputs of receptors of various kinds -- micro-receptors innately existing at the whole-body cellular levels of our species, and which genetically download into every individual of it.

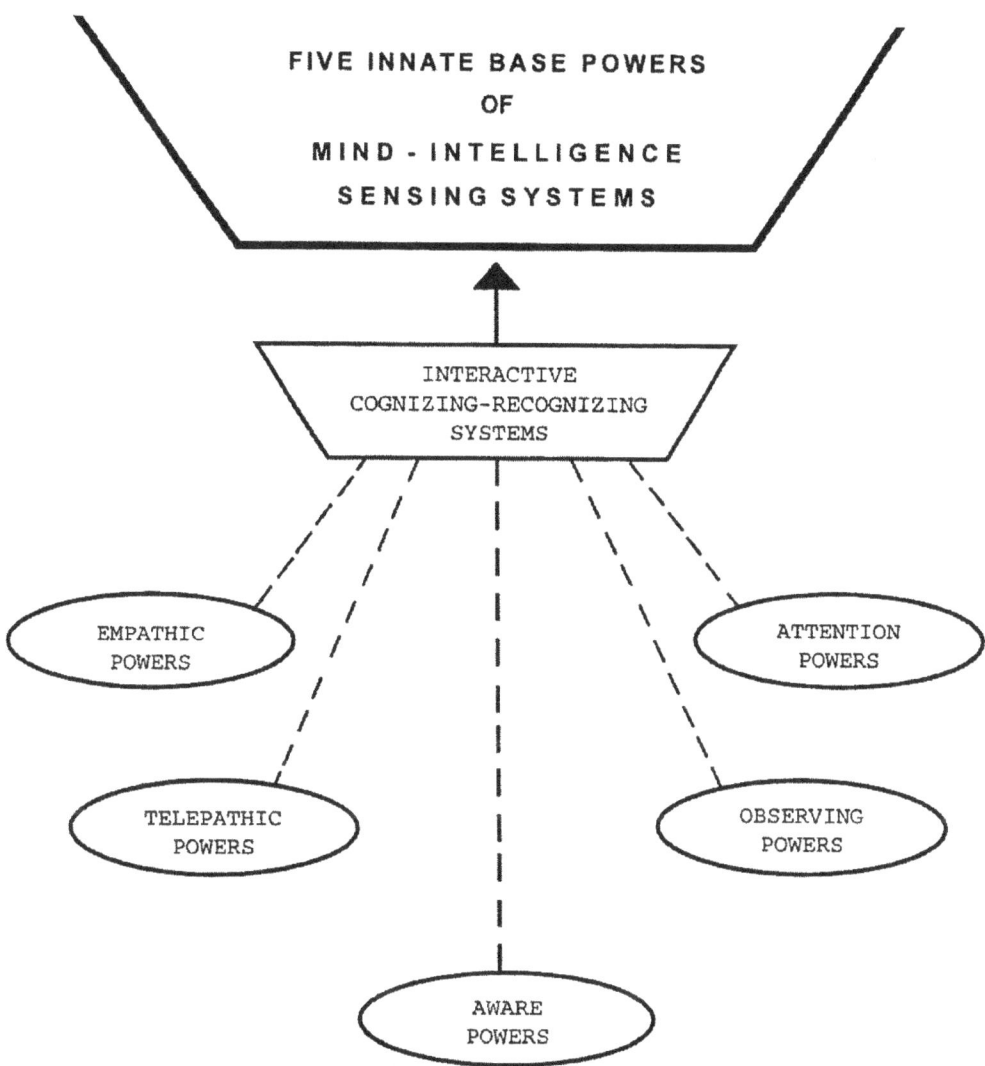

FIGURE 13. Individual mind-intelligence systems possess at least five base powers that detect intangible information impulses. These base powers can be interactive, and all five have something to do with intuition and insight. Without these powers, it is unlikely that mind-intelligence could deduce or interpret anything about physicality except in some very gross tangible format. All five of these powers can be enhanced, but if too enhanced they can "see" what others cannot - and so whether they should be enhanced enters into power games considerations.

Chapter 25

HUMAN POWERS TELEPATHIC

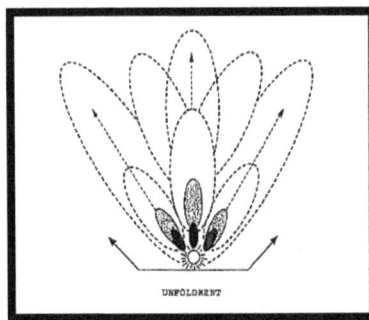

THERE APPEAR to be at least five sets of base human powers that can easily be recognized, although other individuals can probably identify additional ones.

These are the powers empathic and telepathic, the powers of observing, and the aware and attention powers.

These powers can be thought of as fundamental or basic, since altogether they formulate a base upon which additional powers can become active.

Although quite different in obvious and subtle ways, these five sets of base powers have important factors in common.

One factor in common is that if these five base powers are subtracted from the human organism, then the future of the remaining organism is seriously in doubt.

Another common factor is that although the major physical sensing organs are important with respect to these five powers, it is clear that they are more closely associated with receptors that detect and interpret meanings of subtle energies and impulses.

Yet another factor in common is that there are enormous deficits of research information about these five base powers, and this constitutes an impressive knowledge vacuum once it can be recognized as existing.

The existence of this knowledge vacuum can only mean that the five base powers are too closely associated with empowerment and power.

And so any potential real knowledge about them needs to undergo various social and societal management machinations the general goal of which is to prevent discovery of ways and means of enhancing them.

SOCIETAL RESISTENCE AGAINST DEVELOPING KNOWLEDGE ABOUT THE FIVE BASE POWERS

Once it is recognized as such, the absence of research and information with respect to the potentials of human awareness is appalling.

But societal power structures cannot afford to encourage too much empowerment of awareness, since such would seriously make for management difficulties within the larger populations of the powerless or relatively powerless. In fact, dumbed down awareness powers probably equate to depowerment of some kind.

Any in-depth examination of the characteristics of social or societal power structures will reveal that overt and covert efforts are made to prevent accessible accumulations of knowledge about these five base powers.

That they do exist is taken for granted, of course. But research and enlightenment about their full scope of potentials is hardly anywhere to be found.

The principal reason, of course, is that even moderately enhanced powers of empathy, telepathy, observing, awareness, and attention WILL result in recognition of motives and intentions of others.

Thus, these five powers have long been considered as invasive by those informed enough to recognize them as such -- especially invasive with respect to maintenance of power and to power games.

And so any trend toward enlightenment about the five powers can be met with vivid outrage within this or that power structure.

And such has been the clear-cut case in our recent modernist times with respect to the base powers of telepathy. Those powers, known absolutely to exist, have been considered an appropriate topic for parapsychology research, but only by parapsychologists.

Otherwise, and for obvious reasons, such research has not achieved support of any power structure anywhere, excepting some short-term interest on behalf of secret espionage under some kind of power-structure control.

The up-shot of such research is that if powers of telepathy are somehow enhanced, they will be illusive of power-structure control. End of the telepathy story.

THE CONCEPT OF TELEPATHY

The term TELEPATHY was coined sometime before 1882 by the energetic British psychical researcher Frederick William Henry Myers (1843-1901). It was immediately taken up by the British Society for Psychical Research in 1882, and has since come down to us, albeit with several changes in definition.

Among those definitions, the one that caught on and stuck, largely because of media hype, had to do with the idea of one mind broadcasting to another mind, which was soon truncated as "mind-to-mind" and "mind-reading," the latter of which had an earlier history going back some time.

But this mind-to-mind concept did not come about until radio broadcasting was convincingly demonstrated in 1913, after which many conceptualized that mental broadcasting worked like radio broadcasting did.

THIS has never been proven since 1913, but the idea continues to hold a kind of hypnotic sway.

Literally speaking, the prefix TELE is the Greek term for far off, at a distance, across distance, etc.

PATHIC is from the Greek PATHETIKOS, a term having to do with being capable of feeling or capable of evoking.

Literally speaking, then, and in the context meant by Myers in 1882, telepathy is feeling-evoking across distance, or at a distance, etc.

Meyers also coined another term closely related to his concept of telepathy. This was TELETHESIA, a combination of the Greek TELE + AISTHANESTHAI, meaning to perceive -- i.e., perception across distance.

Myers felt that the term telesthesia was needed alongside that of telepathy after it was found that the communications between distant persons is not a transference of thought alone, but of emotions, of motor impulses, and of "many impressions not easy to define."

Many examples of telesthesia were identified. For example, on November 4, 1914, a mother experienced a sharp pain in her arm where there was no wound. With some conviction, she stated that her son, away at war, had just been injured in his arm. Confirmation of this soon arrived by mail.

Myers coined yet another term- - TELERGY -- to name the "force or its mode of action, which is manifest in telepathy, telesthesia, and perhaps in other supernormal operations."

A point must be made here to ensure that FORCE, as a noun, is principally first defined as: "a strength or energy exerted or brought to bear," AND is also synonymous with POWER. (Please note that FORCE, as a verb, has other definitions.)

It is also worth repeating that the definitions of IMPULSE are given as: "(1) the action of stimulating; (2) the act of driving onward with sudden force; (3) a force so communicated as to produce motion, incentive, inspiration, or motivation."

One might wish to memorize the third definition just above, because grounds will shortly be presented that will lead toward wondering if our human sensing systems possess receptors for detecting incentive, inspiration, or motivation of others. The answer will be in the positive.

THOUGHT TRANSFERENCE

Before the term "telepathy" was coined in 1882, the phenomena involved had been referred to as thought transference, sometimes as sympathetic connection, and, more loosely, as mind-reading. Those earlier concepts, especially that of sympathetic connection, can still be applied to telepathic activity.

But the reason for referring to the earlier terms is to remind that the phenomena involved have, in the on-going human framework, existed throughout the ages, and that most languages contained their own terms for them.

The Greek historian, Herodotus (484?-425? B.C.) wrote his HISTORIES during the fifth century B.C. and included in them references to very numerous events that today correspond to empathic powers, to telepathy, and to elegant forms of intuition.

Some two-thousand years later, the famous Swiss physician, Paracelsus (1437-1541), wrote: "By the magic power of the will a person in this side of the ocean, may make a person on the other side hear what is said on this side. The ethereal body of a man may know what another man thinks at a distance of 100 miles or more."

Paracelsus is otherwise famous for helping launch the modern sciences of chemistry and metallurgy, and although he was noted for having a big ego, he was not one to repeat baseless hearsay.

TELEPATHY AS IMPULSE INFORMATION TRANSFER

Regardless of whatever terms are assigned to the phenomena of telepathy, the active principle involved has majorly to do with information transfer among and between living organisms.

This transferring takes place via means other than the interfacing of objective mediums such as talking, writing, or any other kind of external signals.

In other words, the processes of telepathy take place via some kind of direct sensing that does not require anything other than receptors and emitters of information impulses.

And so much depends on whether such receptors exist.

THE DISCOVERY OF TELEPATHY RECEPTORS

Attention is now drawn to items 7, 10, and 12 that were listed in chapter 21, and again provided below for ease of reference.

7. Skin receptors that "recognize" the temperament of other biological organisms.

10. Microsystem transducing of various forms of mechanical, chemical, and electromagnetic energy into meaningful nerve impulses.

12. Neurological receptors for interpreting modulated electronic information by converting it into analog signals for mental storage.

While these three items may seem a bit technical, not to worry because all they really mean is that the human organism possesses receptors that are clearly part of the basis for telepathic reception of raw impulse information.

The direct implication is that such information is converted into meaningful nerve impulses -- whether the individual is consciously aware of it or not.

The direct implication of THAT implication is that the human individual can, in potential at least, consciously recognize the meaning of the nerve impulses providing that one has not become consciously insensitive to them.

But even if one has been educationally conditioned to be consciously insensitive, there is often tendency of telepathic nerve impulses to break through into consciousness anyway -- and so the individual experiences an event of "spontaneous telepathy."

During modern times, many books have been devoted to recording anecdotal evidence of spontaneous telepathy, some of which are listed in the bibliography.

And since the discovery of whole-body and brain receptors that are telepathic-like in nature, new developments along those lines can be found in the Internet under the category of "telepathic receptors."

That the human organism possesses receptors for various kinds of telepathy information transference is now in evidence, not only including mind-to-mind potentials, but a very interesting category referred to as "telepathic osmosis."

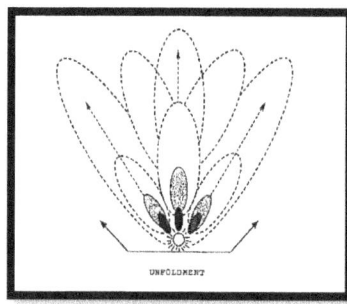

Chapter 26

HUMAN POWERS OF OBSERVING

DURING THE course of 1993, NEWSWEEK magazine, in its June 28 issue, featured an article about "The Puzzle of Genius: New Insights Into Great Minds."

The article was also subtitled "Where Do Great Minds Come From?" -- this being a question that sort of sidestepped the larger issue of where minds come from in the first place.

The major blurb for the article indicated that:

"Scholars have long despaired of even defining genius, let alone identifying its magical ingredients. Now they're beginning to tease out the temperaments, personalities and styles of thought that characterize the Darwins, Mozarts and Napoleons of history. The new insights promise to help ordinary mortals become more creative and to teach schools and parents how to nurture unusual intelligence."

The article was six pages long, and a great deal was briskly discussed in it. But in the end, it was more or less concluded that those having genius were thus and so because they could see what others do not.

That news, not very staggering, was somewhat empty because WHY genius could see, but others could not, was not addressed. Back to square one.

Some clarity might have emerged if seeing what others do not see had at least been connected to issues of human sensing systems, and which are ultimately linked to the spectrum of human powers overall.

And indeed, if one sees what others do not, then one will have attained at least a modicum of power of some kind, whether large or small.

In any event, the question arises concerning why genius sees what others do not.

One possible part of an answer is that genius perceives and/or detects more connections between things than others do -- and takes advantage of them.

For sore clarity here, they do not just see what is out there, or see what is to be seen. They see how things are connected, or how they may or can be connected.

For even more clarity, any number of things can be seen, for example, by the physical senses. But connections between what is seen are not apparent -- until the connections are detected or deduced.

While this statement might seem a little silly at first, the fact remains that seeing things and seeing connections between them are two entirely different matters.

There is a slight nomenclature difficulty in the sentence just above.

Literally speaking, things might be SEEN by everyone in an automatic, eyeballing way. Identifying their connections requires something additional to the mere seeing. This something additional also needs to be more specializing than mere seeing.

There is one conceptualizing term that fills the bill here -- to OBSERVE. And so the fact remains that SEEING things and OBSERVING connections between them are two entirely different matters -- because it is apparent that two different sensing systems are involved.

In this rather roundabout way, we now arrive at the human powers of OBSERVING -- and which, in some dictionaries, ARE actually indicated as powers.

MODERN DEFINITIONS OF OBSERVE

There are three definitions for OBSERVE found in most modern dictionaries:

1. To come to realize or know, especially through consideration of noted facts;
2. To see or sense, especially through directed careful analytic attention;
3. To inspect or take note of as an augury, omen, or presage [please note that this is also one definition of intuition.]

It is useful here to point up that ANALYTIC refers to "separating something into component parts or constituent elements."

OBSOLETE DEFINITIONS OF OBSERVE

The term OBSOLETE is defined as "to grow old; to become disused; no longer in use; outmoded; of a kind or style no longer current."

There exist five pre-modern definitions for OBSERVE that are indicated as obsolete:

To treat with attention or regard;
To attend to with the mind;
To watch for in order to take advantage of;
To examine phenomena as they are presented to the senses;

To examine in order to determine [or, to detect for that matter].

Exactly why these definitions are indicated as obsolete is nowhere made clear or even rational. In any event the obsolete definitions have one essential characteristic that is different from those of the three modern definitions first given above.

The modern definitions do not imply action. Rather, they imply just taking note of something. But the obsolete definitions clearly imply some kind of action -- and where such action is, there is also the potential for some kind of empowerment.

This is especially clear with respect to the third obsolete definition above. For "to watch for in order to take advantage of" something does not mean just taking note of it.

Although it is somewhat baleful to point it up, if one considers the balance between the powerful versus the powerless, it is clear that the powerless are not supposed to observe and watch so as to take advantage of anything.

Indeed, the powerless or depowered are supposed to stay that way. And so, they are neither supposed "to examine in order to determine" or detect, nor "to examine phenomena as they are presented to the senses."

Another overall characteristic of the obsolete definitions is that they tend toward empowerment of those individuals who might not agree that they ARE obsolete and might not give a hoot if they are.

OBSERVING POWERS vis-à-vis SURVIVAL

In the contexts of the foregoing definitions it can become at least somewhat clear that one can SEE what is presented to the senses.

Yet, to merely see what is presented to the senses is, frankly, not enough for survival, getting ahead, getting empowered, or surmounting power competitions.

There is an old adage that one can look at something and not see it; it also turns out that one can see something but not observe it.

It also might be mentioned that detaching the "obsolete" definitions from OBSERVE is some really strange piece of work.

Chapter 27

HUMAN AWARE POWERS

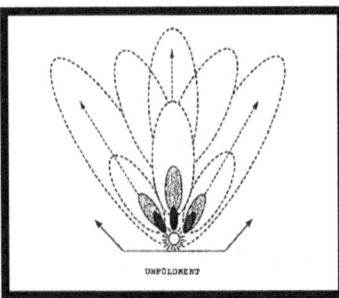

IT IS quite challenging to discuss human aware powers because those powers seem to have been the least identified, examined, and researched.

In that aware powers are everywhere taken for granted, some might not believe there is an enormous paucity of information about them.

This paucity can be discovered in any number and kind of supposedly responsible reference sources, and one can even find that the term is non-existent in some psychological dictionaries.

One could wish simply to ignore this paucity and get on with the business of this volume. But part of the business is to examine depowerment, and to try to identify what it consists of so as to enhance realities leading to empowerment.

So, for starters, it seems necessary to establish the utter importance of human aware powers. And the best way to emphasize this is to use imagination to subtract them from the other constituent elements that comprise our species and its downloaded individuals.

If aware powers are totally subtracted, the end product is something akin to a blob into which the mind, if it CAN exist with this subtraction, has disappeared.

And as everyone can confirm for themselves, even when aware powers are only partially subtracted, one can encounter reality boxes with legs walking around and even trying to do this or that -- perhaps blissfully unaware of being unaware.

Everyone is excellently born with receptors for all sorts of aware powers. And so diminutions of their activity are almost certainly the result of overt and covert social conditioning, at least in some full part. Of course, it is quite important within the contexts of pyramidal power structures that the larger echelons of the powerless should not be aware of too much. And so it is sensible, in those contexts, to not draw attention to ways and means for the multitudes to nurture, enhance, and develop higher and more refined states of their innate aware powers.

IMPORTANT DISTINCTIONS BETWEEN "AWARE" AND "AWARENESS"

The word AWARE entered English over a thousand years ago at about 1095, and was probably taken from Old High German. At that time, it meant: "Wary, alert, watchful, vigilant, cautious, to be on one's guard."

Two hundred years later, at about 1205, a second definition came into existence: "Informed of, cognizant of, conscious of or about something; to have cognizance, to know."

The 1095 definition implies an active principle that is dependent only on itself, i.e., a state of alert in general, a state that can perhaps be thought of as a broadband preparedness alert with respect to WHATEVER.

The 1205 definition implies a passive principle that is associated with or linked to an object, topic, subject, or situation.

During the twentieth century, dictionaries emphasized the second definition, usually phrasing it something like: "Having or showing realization, perception, or knowledge."

Those same dictionaries indicated that the original meanings of "wary, watchful, vigilant, cautious, to be on one's guard" are archaic and obsolete.

Well, it is somewhat difficult to become aware of WHY those original definitions should be thought of as obsolete -- largely because in actuality, and in real life, they can NEVER be obsolete, and should NEVER be thought of as such.

There IS, however, one area of human living within which the action of reducing the original definitions to obsolete irrelevance would be desirable.

That area of course consists of social and societal power structures and competitions in the context of which it would be desirable to REDUCE the original definitions to obsolescence.

The reason for AGAIN repeating this situation is to begin a discussion of a single distinction -- which is very subtle, and so it is necessary to slowly walk through it.

"Having or showing realization, perception, or knowledge" is, of course, one kind of awareness in our contemporary terms, but it is awareness OF or ABOUT something.

For clarity, awareness of or about something has more to do with what the something is -- and in that sense it is the something that determines what the awareness is and/or consists of.

For example, knowledge is not just knowledge, in that it consists of information of various kinds that are packaged as "knowledge."

While one can build awareness OF or ABOUT the packaged information, it is the information that thence packages the parameters of awareness.

A wondrous aspect of information is that it can be manipulated this way or that. It can be erroneous to begin with. It can be falsified and faked, and can be manufactured and/or designed in formats that evoke interest -- but which result in little else.

The suffix -NESS is utilized to indicate a state, condition, quality, or degree of something. It can now be pointed up that "OF or ABOUT something," no matter what it is, is a far cry from the original definition of AWARE -- wary, watchful, vigilant, cautious, to be on one's guard.

Chapter 28

HUMAN ATTENTION POWERS

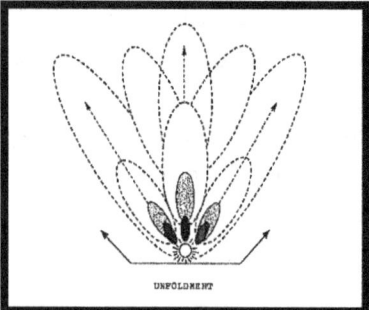

AS HAS been discussed, human empathic, telepathic, observing, and aware powers have NOT undergone research and development during the modern period. Indeed, even definitions for the terms have remained sparse, absent, or confusing, while many of their early substantive meanings have been declared archaic and obsolete.

Please note that telepathy has undergone limited research, but only within the contexts of psychic research and parapsychology -- which fields have not been incorporated into the otherwise conventional sciences, or even into psychology.

It is therefore somewhat surprising to note that the topic of attention has attracted research during the modern period, although the reasons behind this are not exactly clear.

What is clear, however, is that attention is still not identified as a significant human power, and thus the direct connection of attention to empowerment has never been discussed. Most modern dictionaries typically define ATTENTION in two parts:

1. The act or state of attending, especially through applying the mind to an object of sense or thought;
2. A condition of readiness for such attention involving especially a selective narrowing or focusing of consciousness and receptivity.

However, the term ATTENTION is drawn from the term ATTEND which is taken from the Latin word AD + TENDERE, which is defined as "to stretch to" something. Hence the earliest English definition, circa 1300, is given as "to direct the eyes, ears, mind, energies to anything."

Now, in the most literal sense, "to stretch TO" means exactly that -- to reach out, to direct toward, as if to touch or include.

One of the most interesting facets of the early definition is the inclusion of "energies" in it. On the surface, this does not make too much sense. But there is a familiar phenomenon many experience, a phenomenon known from ancient times, having to do with focusing attention on the back of another's head, and having that head turn around to look-see who or what.

Indeed, the ancient Greeks thought that the eyes had the power of focusing a kind of energy power and stretching it out until it touched someone in some energetic way sufficient enough to call forth some kind of response.

Although it is still not well known, between 1925 and the fall of the Soviet Union, this phenomenon was tested within the contexts of Soviet bio-information transfer research not only between individuals in sight of each other, but across larger distances. The attention stretching-out phenomenon was found to exist in both the near and far aspects.

Indeed, if telepathy phenomena exist over distances, then the attention-stretching-out thing must also exist.

The inclusion of "energies" in the early definitions of ATTEND-ATTENTION preserves the active energetic component of attention. It is this active energetic component that qualifies and distinguishes a human power.

Against this active energetic context, the two contemporary definitions given earlier can be seen as relatively passive in nature. And indeed, the "focusing of consciousness and receptivity" establishes as much.

Of course, passive receptivity is also a power, but it has to do with input, or intake, of information about whatever attention gets focused on.

The stretching-out type of attention is an output of some kind, and if the energies involved are focused and have strength, the stretching-out equates, fair and square, to a power PROJECTION.

Like human powers of awareness, the human powers of attention are two-fold, i.e., passive and active, intake and output.

POWERS OF ATTENTION

ACTIVE ATTENTION . . . . PASSIVE ATTENTION
Output, emitter   Input, receptor

Some dictionaries of psychological terms identify ATTENTION as "the process of preferentially responding to a stimulus or range of stimuli; the adjustment of the sense organs and central nervous system for maximal stimulation."

Edward B. Titchener (1867-1927), who, from 1910, was head of the New Psychological Laboratory at Cornell University, established several factors regarding attention, and offered that it was "a state of sensory clearness with a margin and a focus."

Titchener also coined the term ATTENSITY -- meaning sensory clearness -- a term that seems not to have caught on, The PSYCHIATRIC DICTIONARY (compiled by Robert J. Campbell, 5th Ed., 1981) defines ATTENTION as "Conscious and willful focusing of mental energy on one object or one component of a complex experience and at the same time excluding other emotional or thought content."

One researcher, Kenneth Nakdimen, sought to establish that the left and right hemisphere of the brain have different types of attention.

He suggested that ALLOPLASTIC ATTENTION is mainly a function of the left hemisphere -- it is analytic-conceptualizing-abstracting; it is characterized by maintenance of ego boundaries; and it includes that form of attention to attention that is commonly called REFLECTION.

AUTOPLASTIC ATTENTION, on the other hand, is a function of the right hemisphere; it is gestalt-imaging-concretizing attention that is synesthetic and self-altering; it is characterized by diffusion of ego boundaries; and it includes that form of attention called IMAGINATION. (Bulletin of the Menninger Clinic, 42, 1978.)

PLASTIC refers to whatever is capable of being continuously and permanently stretched, worked, molded, malleable, or pliable without rupturing.

The prefix ALLO- refers to "other, outside of, external to." Thus, alloplastic attention results from stimuli (impulses) input from outer world, and which shape and determine what the resulting awareness consists of — i.e., passive awareness.

The prefix AUTO- refers to whatever originates within the individual independently of outside influence and of normal trains and models of thought.

In this sense, AUTOGENIC refers to "whatever originates within self, or is self-generated, independent of external stimuli."

AUTOGENIC GESTALT refers to "a perceptual unity arising from innate factors as opposed to stimulus factors."

Along these same lines, AUTOGENIC REINFORCEMENT refers to "the strengthening of a response by factors innate in the organism so that the resulting response is stronger than could be accounted for by stimulating conditions only." I.e., perhaps by innate power factors as discussed in chapter 20.

Chapter 29

HUMAN PROJECTING POWERS

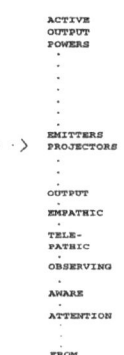

ACTIVE
OUTPUT
POWERS
.
.
.
EMITTERS
PROJECTORS
.
OUTPUT
EMPATHIC
TELE-
PATHIC
OBSERVING
.
AWARE
ATTENTION

FROM
SELF TO
OTHERS

A FULL part of any empowerment principle ultimately must include considerations having to do with extending influence with respect to active situations and circumstances within which one finds oneself.

After all, whatever else it might consist of, life is an activity, and any life organisms must in some sense be innately and naturally equipped to interact with life activity. If not, the survival principle diminishes or vanishes accordingly.

At the human species level, the species mind-intelligence systems apparently seem "designed" not only to interact with active life situations and circumstances, but also to influence and transcend them as they change and shift about.

At the human individual level, however, individuals are incorporated into active social and societal situations and circumstances, often a large number of them.

These are characterized by various kinds of lesser or greater pyramidal power structures within which distinctions between the powerful, the less powerful, and the powerless are usually trenchantly demarcated -- and which, furthermore, are based on firm historical precedents that are emphasized as having been important to human "development."

If, as can be suspected from copious evidence, the human species is a power species both in principle and in design, then who or what is to have influence within power contexts will always constitute a focal point with whatever situations and circumstances come into existence.

Our English term INFLUENCE is taken from the Latin IN + FLUERE defined as "to flow." But the English term also includes the context of "emanating," i.e., from whence the flowing emanates.

Thus, INFLUENCE (as the verb) has three principal definitions: To affect or alter by indirect or intangible means; To have an effect on the condition or development of something; To modify.

There can be little doubt that the human power species has powers of setting up power structures, and so history is loaded with different formats of them.

The formats might differ in detail. But as again stated, central to all of them is who or what is to have emanating influence.

In the typical power structure, the influence usually is accepted as emanating from the top, with the powers of EMANATING it becoming lesser and lesser downward into its larger populations who are really supposed to NOT emanate too much. Hence, the so-called power-less usually do not or cannot influence too much either.

The term EMANATE is taken from the Latin E + MANARE, defined as "to come out from a source." If the human species is to wheel and deal in active influencing as vastly as it does, then that species is innately equipped to put out, or to project, influences of numerous kinds.

Additionally, influences cannot become influences unless they are somehow sensed or detected as such -- and so the species must be innately equipped with receptors and detectors that are sensitive to influences.

Yet, influences cannot be felt as such unless they are first emanated, or emitted, or projected from some sources. And so the basic human equipment regarding influencing MUST involve emitters as well as receptors.

As it is, however, power structures cannot have too many of their inhabitants running around actively emitting or projecting too much on their own.

And so over time, and very early, the best discovered way of preventing this is to conceal information and knowledge that individuals of the species are equipped with emitters and powers of projecting.

And indeed, there is a nomenclature history demonstrating that something like this has been underway for some time.

THE REALITY OF THE POWERS OF PROJECTING

During the late modern period, the term PROJECT as the verb, not the noun, was defined as: "to devise in the mind; to throw something or cast it forward; to present for consideration characteristic of; to cause to protrude; to communicate vividly, especially to an audience; to externalize and regard as objective or outside of oneself."

However, the term PROJECT entered ENGLISH at about 1430 It was taken from the Latin PROJECTUS meaning "to stretch out, to throw forth, to extend."

All three of these definitions were accepted into English back then -- and all three of them are now indicated as obsolete.

At about 1600, another definition came into existence, i.e., "to plan, devise, or design TO DO something." [Please note that the emphasis on TO DO is found in the Oxford dictionary.] This definition is today indicated as "rare or obsolete."

At about the same time, another definition came into usage: "To put forth, set forth, exhibit; to present to expectation." This definition is today indicated as obsolete.

RADIATE: to send out rays; to spread abroad as if from a center.
EMANATE: to come out from a source; to give out; to emit; to flow out.
EMIT: to throw or give off or out; to put into circulation;
PROJECT: "to stretch out; to throw forth; to extend."

```
PASSIVE                                              ACTIVE
INTAKE                                               OUTPUT
POWERS                                               POWERS
  .                                                    .
  .                                                    .
  .                                                    .
  .                                                    .
  .                                                    .
  .                   S E L F                          .
  .                                                    .
RECEPTORS          P O W E R                       EMITTERS
DETECTORS  · · · · >              · · · · >        PROJECTORS
  .                F U L C R U M                       .
  .                                                    .
  .                                                    .
INPUT                                                OUTPUT
  .                                                    .
EMPATHIC                                             EMPATHIC
  .                                                    .
TELE-                                                TELE-
PATHIC                                               PATHIC
  .                                                    .
OBSERVING                                            OBSERVING
  .                                                    .
AWARE                                                AWARE
  .                                                    .
ATTENTION                                            ATTENTION
  .                                                    .
  .                                                    .
FROM                                                 FROM
OTHERS TO                                            SELF TO
SELF                                                 OTHERS
```

<u>FIGURE 14</u>. The function of the above tentative diagram is to display the probability that all of the five base powers can be emitted or projected as well as received or detected. It is quite probable that each of the base powers somehow interacts with each other. Something like this is undeniably the case with the empathic and telepathic powers, and it is generally understood that higher states of awareness in a given individual can stimulate and attract the awareness and attention of others. All individuals do have self power fulcrums, but it is understood that their vitalization ratio might depend on any number of factors realized or not realized.

PART FIVE
THE REAL EXISTENCE OF HUMAN GROKING POWERS

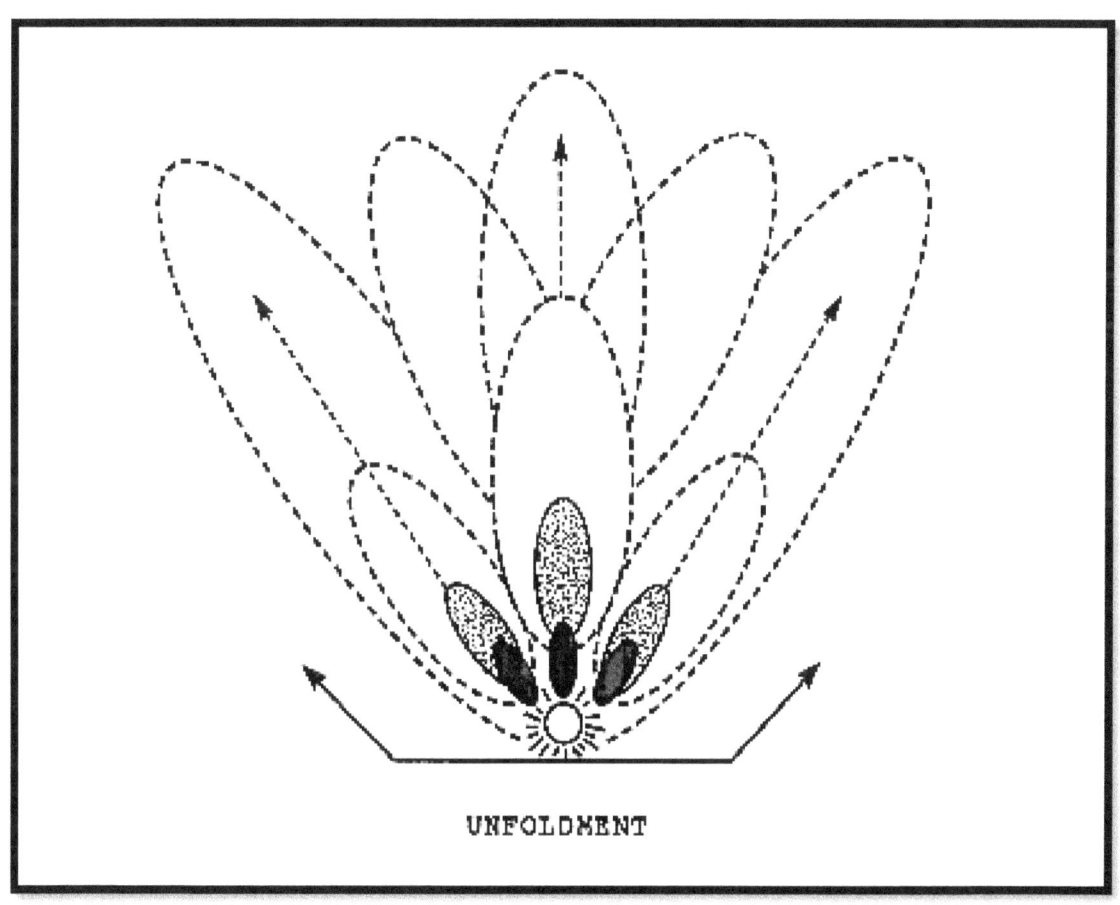

UNFOLDMENT

Chapter 30

GETTING BEYOND LIMITATIONS OF REALITY BOXES AND LANGUAGE SYSTEMS

PERMEABLE

Expanded or empowered thresholds of human innate base powers

May be capable of sourcing beyond self

EMPOWERMENT CAN be considered within the contexts of various types of reality boxes.

For example, empowerment can indeed be thought of in the contexts of achieving authority, influence, and control over others.

This trinity personifies societal power in such strong ways that it makes it seem the only real form of power. And so reality boxes reflecting it are endlessly replicated, cloned, and passed down through the generations.

Even so, it can be wondered if the human organism with all of its amazing powers, attributes, and faculties, came into existence simply to adapt to societal power structures, and which adapting requires the deadening of many powers in so many individuals.

This is especially to be wondered about, largely because social and societal power structures arise and vanish, disappearing into a history that sometimes does not even record them. Also to be noted is the fact that societal power struggles can consume the powerful as well as the powerless, and it is certain that the days and times of the socially triumphant powerful are as numbered as anything transitory is.

Anyone who studies human power(s) deeply enough will sooner or later come to realize that humans not only possess identified powers that are latent and not energized, but also powers that have never been identified so as to have words assigned to them.

For example, there are at least twenty different types of telepathy that could be recognized as such. There are several types of empathic activity, and, for that matter, quite a few types of awareness and intuition. These types have not yet been recognized and discriminated from each other, and so there are no words or terms for them.

It is important to consider this because if words are not assigned to something, then it is almost impossible to verbally discuss or write about it. This is almost the same as saying, as many semantic experts do, that if a thing has not achieved a linguistic term, then it doesn't exist - at least as language systems go.

Bearing this in mind, there now arises something that is very seldom considered.

Well over 30,000-plus human languages are known to have existed, plus X-numbers of languages that have been lost to posterity, plus languages for which evidence exists, but which have resisted decoding and translation.

This brings up a two-part wonderment as to whether human powers exist prior to the invention of linguistic terms for them -- or do the powers come into existence only after they have been assigned a linguistic identity.

The second part of this wonderment seems a little stupid, because it can roughly be assumed that humans do not in general invent linguistic terms for something they have not experienced as real enough to deserve establishing a linguistic identify for it.

Indeed, for a linguistic term to be useful it all, it has to point or refer to something that can be recognized at least in some basic way and recognized independently of linguistic terms.

In fact, 30,000 different languages can produce 30,000 different words for something that is generally experienced by everyone, no matter which language they come to utilize.

So, in fundamental essence, experiencing something and recognizing that it has been experienced comes before assigning a nomenclature term to it.

One of the points being made here is that the human species as a whole possesses innate powers, all of which exist before a language system is set up to assign terms to the powers.

The term INNATE is defined as:

1. Existing in or belonging to an individual from birth;
2. Belonging to the essential nature of something;
3. Originating in or derived from the mind or the constitution of the intellect rather than from experience.

It is worth emphasizing definition (3) just above i.e., derived from mind-intelligence rather than from experience, possibly derived even BEFORE experience, and in which case derived before terms can be invented and assigned.

HARD DRIVES OF HUMAN MIND-INTELLIGENCE

INNATE can also be compared to a computer hard drive which must exist before software programs can be inserted.

This concept of hard drives can be extended to include all of the systems innate in each human organism, each of which pre-exist subsequent shaping by the equivalent of software programs - such as, for example, those of social conditioning.

The existence of at least some human innate hard drives has been discovered. In its July 1993 issue, LIFE magazine featured an elegant article entitled "The Amazing Minds of Infants."

This article brought together the findings of various researchers originally focusing on how infants begin to learn whatever they do.

But one of the major outcomes of the research had to do with ascertaining in infants the existence of "innate abilities we're just beginning to understand."

"Innate," of course, refers to "born with," or "already born with," as contrasted to being acquired at some point down the line.

One such innate, born-with, factor has to do with estimation that "babies are universal linguists capable of distinguishing each of the 150 sounds that make up all human speech," and thus make up all human languages in one way or another.

For clarity here, each human individual comes pre-equipped with a hard drive module that deals with the 150 sounds that make up all languages -- and into which can be input the software programs of one or more of the 30,000 languages known to exist or to have existed.

Other innate hard drives found in infants have to do with the amazing extent of their inborn powers of memory and, of all things, for math -- for infants can begin to add and subtract before they learn to count.

One of the conclusions of the LIFE article was that "Researchers now know that babies are anything but blank slates. You can tell that wheels are turning. They're paying attention to the world in incredibly subtle ways."

And, as the whole of the LIFE article implies, they are doing so with powers already innate rather than later acquired through conventional ideas about what "learning" consists of.

As of this writing, Internet search engines reveal over 15,000 references having to do with "Babies are smarter than you think," many of which point out rather amazing powers of infants.

HUMAN HARD DRIVE SUBTLE ROWERS

Modern definitions for the term SUBTLE are given as "delicate, refined, mentally acute, keen, highly skillful, expert, cunning, ingenious, artful, crafty, and etc."

With these definitions we suddenly encounter a whole spate of qualities that are clearly applicable to people, and all of which can be associated with empowerment and with societal power, and with power games and machinations as well.

However, when the term SUBTLE entered English at about 1390, its first definition was: "Not dense; thin, tenuous, fluidic, penetrating."

Today, there are various easily recognizable definitions for the term PENETRATE and so everyone has something of a general idea of what it means.

But there are two modern definition that seem to have gone somewhat out of use:

"to pierce something with the eye or mind; and to affect deeply the senses or feelings."

There is one modern definition of PENETRATION that is remarkable with regard to human power(s), and which is here exactly quoted: "the power to penetrate, specifically the ability to discern deeply and acutely."

In this sense, however, the ability would constitute a honed or polished skill based on the fundamental or base power(s) of penetrating.

There is more involved here. The term PENETRATE entered into English rather late, at about 1530. It was taken from the Latin PENETRARE, which meant "to place within, enter within, pierce."

The early definition was closely related to PENITUS INTERIOR -- meaning "innermost, to the innermost recesses, to enter and diffuse itself though, to permeate, to imbue with something."

HUMAN SUBTLE POWERS THAT EXIST INDEPENDENT OF NOMENCLATURE FOR THEM

Returning now to the question of whether human powers can exist before nomenclature is invented for them, it is quite clear that they do.

For example, the innate powers of language-making preexist the 30,000-plus languages made, and if the human species and its individuals did not have this innate, hard drive power, then it is doubtful that languages would be erected.

As discussed within the LIFE magazine article referred to above, infants begin "learning" languages BEFORE they learn the words -- a process that some researchers think is achieved by, of all things, a type of "telepathic osmosis."

In this sense, then, our 30,000-plus languages are obviously some kind of software programs that are inserted into the power-innate hard drives, and which themselves already contain recognition patterns for the 150 sounds that make up all languages.

From all of the foregoing, it can be thought that humans possess innate powers that exist whether or not linguistic terms are erected for them, in much the same way that they can exist whether or not organized information about them is included in reality boxes.

HUMAN GROKING POWERS

The English language does not contain a term that refers to human powers that exist and FUNCTION independently of any word-based systems. For that matter, neither do any of the more modern formats of Western language systems.

Some older African and Asian languages do have them, as do some pre-modern languages such as the Hawaiian Huna, the Australian aboriginal, and the Native American languages.

Those other language terms, however, cannot be translated into English because English does not have a term that is equivalent to them.

This author has therefore seized upon the slang term GROK which, although of rather recent vintage, carries the meaning of knowing things in the absence of how or why the knowing should exist or be achieved, and in the absence of words that might otherwise bring linguistic illumination of some kind.

The exact frame of reference being sought for here has to do with information that "comes in" and which cannot, in any basic way, be ascribed to anything one has known or experienced before -- and which, furthermore, does not need words in order to be understood or accepted as real.

The term GROK, as a so-called "arbitrary formation," was coined by Robert A, Heinlein in his famous 1961 science-fiction novel, STRANGER IN A STRANGE LAND.

In dictionaries of slang, it is defined as "to empathize or communicate sympathetically."

Extended common usage of it has also come to refer to the sense of knowing MEANING of things, without bothering with the details of how or why it has come about.

It is important here to emphasize knowing MEANING of things, rather than merely understanding the things themselves.

In support of this distinction, it is rather common knowledge that one might understand things, but not at all grasp their meanings, especially with respect to their larger pictures.

In a certain sense, then, GROK refers to acquiring meaning via empathic, sympathetic, or telepathic powers in formats that are independent of words.

It is fair to point up that the English terms INSPIRED, INSIGHT, INTUITION, COGNITION, and even SENSING per se, are quite near the term GROK, largely because those terms refer to some kind of meaning.

But the chances are very good that those terms refer to various kinds of groking -- i.e., meaning-making independent of the linguistic limits of language.

SOME DISTINCTIONS BETWEEN

PERMEABLE & NOT PERMEABLE

REALITY BOXES

NOT
PERMEABLE

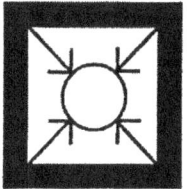

Reduced or
depowered
thresholds
of human
innate base
powers

May be
incapable of
sourcing
beyond self

PERMEABLE

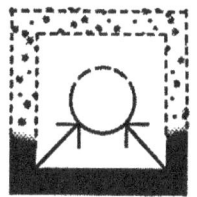

Expanded or
empowered
thresholds
of human
innate base
powers

May be
capable of
sourcing
beyond self

FIGURE 15. As with just about everything else, the permeability or not of reality boxes can always be a matter of degree, and much can also depend on what one does or does not wish to learn, to know about, or to experience. In the end, though, reality boxes are only as good as the information they contain and the functions they serve, and then for only as long as they do.

Chapter 31

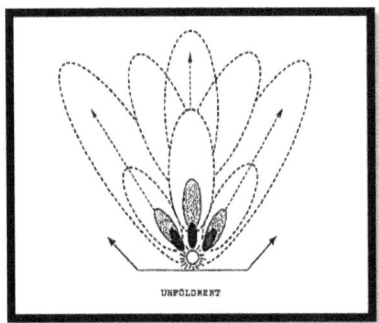

HUMAN POWERS OF GROKING SIGNIFICANCE AND IMPORTANCE

IT IS obvious, or at least it ought to be, that the processes of empowerment are closely involved with recognizing importance.

And it is for this exact reason that whatever has real importance is usually not made too public and can even be encapsulated in layers of secrecy that are difficult to penetrate -- except, possibly, by powers telepathic.

There are two basic ways of considering this.

First, it is quite understandable that the societal powerful will think that whatever has real importance belongs in their territory. And so one of the better definitions of power has to do with having authority, influence, and control not merely over others, but also over what is really important.

Second, those seeking empowerment, but who cannot identify, detect, or grok real importances, are likely to attempt the empowerment within the realms of what is not really important. This can end up with much noisy spinning of wheels, and a lot of such wheel spinning does go on.

In order to get somewhat beyond this situation, it is necessary to examine the modern and pre-modern definitions of the term IMPORTANCE and IMPORTANT.

Most modern dictionaries define IMPORTANT as "marked by or possessing weight or consequence."

IMPORTANCE is thusly defined as: "the quality or state of being important" with regard to "consequence, weight, moment, and significance."

However, the term IMPORTANT came into English at some point between 1450 and 1580, and was taken from the Latin IMPORTANS. The early English definition copied the Latin one of: "to be of consequence, weight, or FORCE" [emphasis added here.] And so it becomes visible that the element of FORCE has been deleted from the modern definitions. This deletion erases the ACTIVE component or element from the modernist definition, leaving behind only the more or less passive contexts.

Consequences have their importances, of course. When and if they do come about they are the result of something that has already happened -- past-oriented, so to speak.

The element of FORCE, however, makes things happen, or at least things are likely to happen via that element, and so the force part of importance is future-oriented.

Since it is not unusual to find that the societal powerful wish to develop or enforce the important future in their own important terms, it is convenient to delete the force element from the public definitions of important and importance.

If the element of force is excluded from definitions of importance, then any number of things can be conceptualized as important, if only to participate in them so as to have the feeling of being important.

On average, this is all well and good enough, for it at least can occupy time between physical birth and death, and even a false-importance serves for that purpose.

And so there are importances that are not really important, and there are importances that are important only as long as this or that individual thinks they are.

From all of the above, one might download the wonderment about how to figure out what is important from among the ever-ongoing plentitude of importances that are not so important.

Modern definitions of the term SIGNIFY are rather simply given as: "to indicate, denote, mean, and imply."

Thus, modern definitions for the term SIGNIFICANCE are: "having meaning, especially suggestive or expressive; suggesting or containing a disguised or special meaning; essential to the determination of some larger element."

It is broadly understood that the way or method of determining the real importance of any given importance is to evaluate its significance.

And as discussed at some length in Volume I, there is something of an amusing scramble involved in all this -- largely because like importances, significance as considered through its modern definitions, can be attributed to importances that are not really significant.

The term SIGNIFY entered English at about 1250, and was taken from the Latin terms SIGNIFICARE and SIGUUM which carried the descriptive definitions of: "to betoken, foreshow, foreshadow, to indicate as something that will take place."

From these early, and original, definitions of SIGNIFY (hence SIGNIFICANCE), it can be recognized that the real importance of any given importance might be recognized by whatever it betokens, foreshows, foreshadows, and indicates that something will take place.

Thus, in the sense of the original definitions, what a given importance signifies in terms of what will take place because of it, largely determines the distinctions between an important importance and an importance that does not signify too much of anything.

Now, to get somewhere near the bottom line of all this, it is unthinkable that a species having innate high-stage intelligence systems would not have innate powers that recognize, cognize, and predict what something signifies -- which is to say, what will take place.

Such powers are groking powers fair and square, but even if one doesn't want to utilize the term GROKING, they are still what-will-happen powers that anyway have to be groked no matter what the groking is called.

Chapter 32

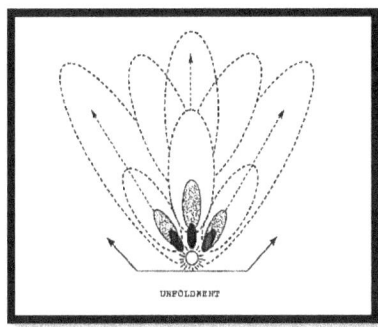

HUMAN GROKING POWERS OF EXPERIENCING

MANY THINKERS who examine human nature have concluded that our experiences provide the basic foundations of what we become.

The reason given in general is that we can perceive only what we experience, and that it is what we experience that shapes or conditions not only what we become, but also our resulting behavior.

This particular information package has acted as a reality box and has led many to assume that our powers of experiencing are the first and foremost of all our powers.

At one level of REAL reality, it is difficult to argue too much against this information package, because it can be applied with logic and success to many situations.

Even so, if other significant factors are brought into consideration, then that information package starts to wobble.

To start with, there are no less than three factors that need to be illuminated, the first of which is that our powers of experiencing are clearly based upon a number of other powers.

And so the powers of experiencing, as important as they are, cannot actually be the first and foremost of human powers.

A second, more serious factor is that the foregoing information package, as described, does not accord very well with the established definitions of EXPERIENCE.

While it is clear enough that notions of experiencing can be what this or that reality box thinks they are, it is obvious that other reality boxes might have other notions for it.

Third, it is a known fact that some experience what others either do or cannot, and vice versa.

And it is also well understood that there are entire squads and even entire social orders of individuals who do not experience what they COULD if numerous of their innate powers had not been put to sleep via social conditioning and various kinds of group and peer pressures.

In any event, the definitions of the term can be divided, as we by now expect, into modern and pre-modern definitions. Thus, the modern definitions are:

1. The usual conscious perception or apprehension of reality or of an external, bodily, or psychic event.
2. Facts or events or the totality of factors or events observed.
3. Direct participation in events.
4. The conscious events that make up an individual life.
5. Something personally encountered, undergone, or lived through.

Based upon the modern definitions above, the definition for EXPERIENCED is given as "made skillful or wise through observation of or participation in events."

Well now! Many experience what they cannot sort out or understand in the contexts of their given reality boxes, and very many more participate in events that totally elude rationality and are completely mystifying.

And as has been mentioned in Part Two, especially in chapter 13, the so-called conscious part of the mind is not a very big one.

It is now useful to dig up the original, pre-modern, definitions in order to point out a significant difference, or shift of meaning, that has taken place.

The term EXPERIENCE entered into English at about 1388, and was taken from the Latin EXPERIENTA, meaning, "to attempt, to try."

The early English definition is given as: "The action of putting to the test; to make trial of; to MAKE experience of."

In about 1391, an additional definition appeared: "Proof by actual trial; practical demonstration; to put IN experience."

By about 1483, EXPERIENCE was defined as: "The state of having been occupied in any department of study or practice, in affairs generally, or in the intercourse of life; the extent to which, or the length of time during which, one has been so occupied; the aptitudes, skill, judgment, etc. thereby acquired."

In about 1563, yet another nuance came into usage: "The actual observation of facts or events, considered as a source of knowledge."

It can now be seen that, as time went on, the original definitions of EXPERIENCE (attempt, try) were transferred over to the word EXPERIMENT.

Another slight departure from the original definitions had to do with "observation as a source of knowledge," and which became attributable to experiment, but not to experience.

By about 1615, EXPERIENCE began to be exclusively defined as "The fact of being consciously the subject of a state or condition, or being consciously affected by an event. A state or condition viewed subjectively. An event by which one is affected."

Via this definition, one can see that "being subject of" and "being affected by" mostly refer to PASSIVE receptivity.

And the five modernist definitions listed earlier reflect the passive, in-take, nature of experiencing -- and give no hint that experiencing has an active side.

One of the conceptual difficulties that interferes with identifying the active side of experiencing is that the modernist definitions conceptualize it entirely as an affair confined exclusively WITHIN the conscious mind part of the individual.

If, however, we consult the original definition of EXPERIENCE, we find that it was first defined as "attempt, try."

The English term ATTEMPT was taken from the Latin AD + TEMPTARE which, literally translated, refers to TOWARD TOUCH.

Here we once more find ourselves in the vicinity of the human "stretching powers" already discussed -- for example, our empathic, telepathic, and intuitional powers, and especially our groking powers.

While it is abundantly obvious that we can passively experience what we are exposed to, it can equally be the case that we can experience what we actively toward-touch.

Another way of approaching what is involved here is to observe that if human mind-intelligence systems could only passively experience what was encountered from the outside, then it is unlikely that human mind-intelligence systems would have no active powers whatsoever.

Indeed, the existence of human intelligence would become questionable, and the human organism would be reduced to the level of all other stimulus-response organisms.

Although it might seem a bit redundant to pump it yet once more, it ought to be obvious that human power structures based on authority, influence, and control of others do not want human toward-touch, stretching out, and groking powers either to be acknowledged as such, and certainly do not wish enhancement of them among one and all.

Experiencing as active toward-touching simply means that one can experience with and what others are experiencing. And here it might be worth mentioning, that toward-touch-experiencing might be one of the fundamental constituents of all REAL humanitarian endeavors.

In any event, the mantra of "Reach out and touch one another," falls somewhere in this category.

Chapter 33

HUMAN GROKING POWERS OF COGNIZING

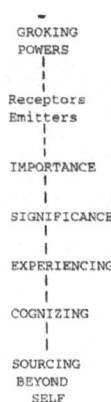

ALL INDIVIDUALS of the human species have innate powers of understanding, which, in part, are closely related to the powers of comprehending.

In most dictionaries, UNDERSTANDING is briskly defined as: "the power to make experience intelligible by applying concepts and categories; to have a clear idea."

COMPREHEND is defined as: "the act or action of grasping with the intellect; the capacity for understanding." But that term stresses the mental processes in arriving at an understanding.

An example of the two distinctions, given in some dictionaries, is "He understood the instructions without comprehending their purpose."

One can also say: "He made his experiences intelligible without comprehending their meaning."

Even though these two terms identify different mental phenomena, they are utilized as synonyms -- for example, understanding is defined as the power of comprehending, and the power of comprehending is defined as understanding.

So there is little wonder that various confusions exist about them. But it is rather safe to indicate that two sets of powers are involved.

Somewhere between the concepts of understand and comprehend is a third category of powers -- the powers of cognizing -- and which, on behalf of any kind of empowerment, must be examined very closely.

There is at least one principal reason for this.

As great as they can be, understanding and comprehending nevertheless can be derived from within the limitations of this or that reality box.

A basic fact is that everyone is born into some kind of environmental, social, and societal reality box, and thereafter understanding and comprehending can be conditioned so that they do not exceed the limits and contours of those reality boxes.

Indeed, societal power structures obtain inclusive control of their populations simply by controlling the contours and limits of understanding and comprehending -- this being one definition of social conditioning.

If the contours and limits of understanding and comprehending are to be effective within societal control systems (whether large or small), then in general the powers of cognizing must not undergo too much support and nurturing. Instead, those powers must undergo this or that kind of depowerment.

The basic reason for this is that the powers of cognizing refer to the acquisition of knowledge, new knowledge, which is external to what one already understands or comprehends.

In English, COGNITION is taken from the Latin COGNOSCERE meaning "to come to know, or to become acquainted with."

From this, the English definition is rendered as: "the act or process of knowing including both awareness and judgment."

The term AWARENESS is not included in definitions of understanding and comprehending. Indeed, those processes can take place without the involvement of too much awareness, and just about anyone can observe various ongoing examples of this.

Furthermore, COGNITION is associated with a "range of apprehension, observing, noticing, perception, and distinguishing accompanied by surveillance and control," all of which work to bring together and unfold elements of KNOWING that are "new" with respect to one's reality box.

The synonym given for COGNIZE is AWARE.

In its purest sense, COGNITION means to become aware of something that one was not aware of before, usually, but not always, by suddenly realizing how things fit together.

And this implies that having a cognition means that one has gone beyond the limits of any former understanding or comprehending.

In principle then, our powers of cognizing refer to information and knowledge not already present within one's reality box -- and which, if experienced, probably will shift and enlarge the contents of reality boxes.

Thus, our powers of cognizing permit us to alter our reality box adaptations upon which all our former understandings and comprehensions have been based.

Now, it must be pointed out that no one has the faintest idea of how and why cognitions can occur, or, for that matter, how and why realizations take place.

But it is generally understood that people have them, and it is also comprehended that if the powerless are to remain as such, then they should not be encouraged to have too many realizations, and certainly as few cognitions as possible.

In order to better grok what is involved here, it is helpful to realize that there are subtle but important differences between the concepts of understanding, comprehending, cognizing, and knowing.

It is obvious that these four powers are connected somehow, and that cognizing and knowing are very closely interconnected.

But the term KNOW is derived from the Latin terms GNOSCERE and NOSCERE that had three equally acceptable meanings: "to know," "to come to know," and "to recognize."

The English term RECOGNIZE is drawn from the Latin RE + COGNOSCERE which, literally translated, meant "again know," are "return-know." Emphasis here is on AGAIN, and which literally means "return anew."

To RE-COGNIZE thus carries the rather amazing idea of knowing again what was once known before -- and the process of achieving this again-knowing can be referred to as achieving a cognition.

The whole of this is, of course, somewhat dizzy-making and one can begin to wonder what the point is.

Well, the point is pointing toward a special category of human mind-intelligence powers that might be called, for lack of a better term, automatic knowing -- a type of knowing that is auto-generated within individual aware systems without recourse to anything external.

The closest terms in English are DIRECT intuition, DIRECT perception, DIRECT understanding and/or comprehension. DIRECT, of course, is defined as "immediate, uninterrupted," with the nuance of getting where one is going without anything intervening.

Direct automatic knowing might also be referred to as SUPERGROKING, but one doesn't wish to push the nomenclature envelope too far.

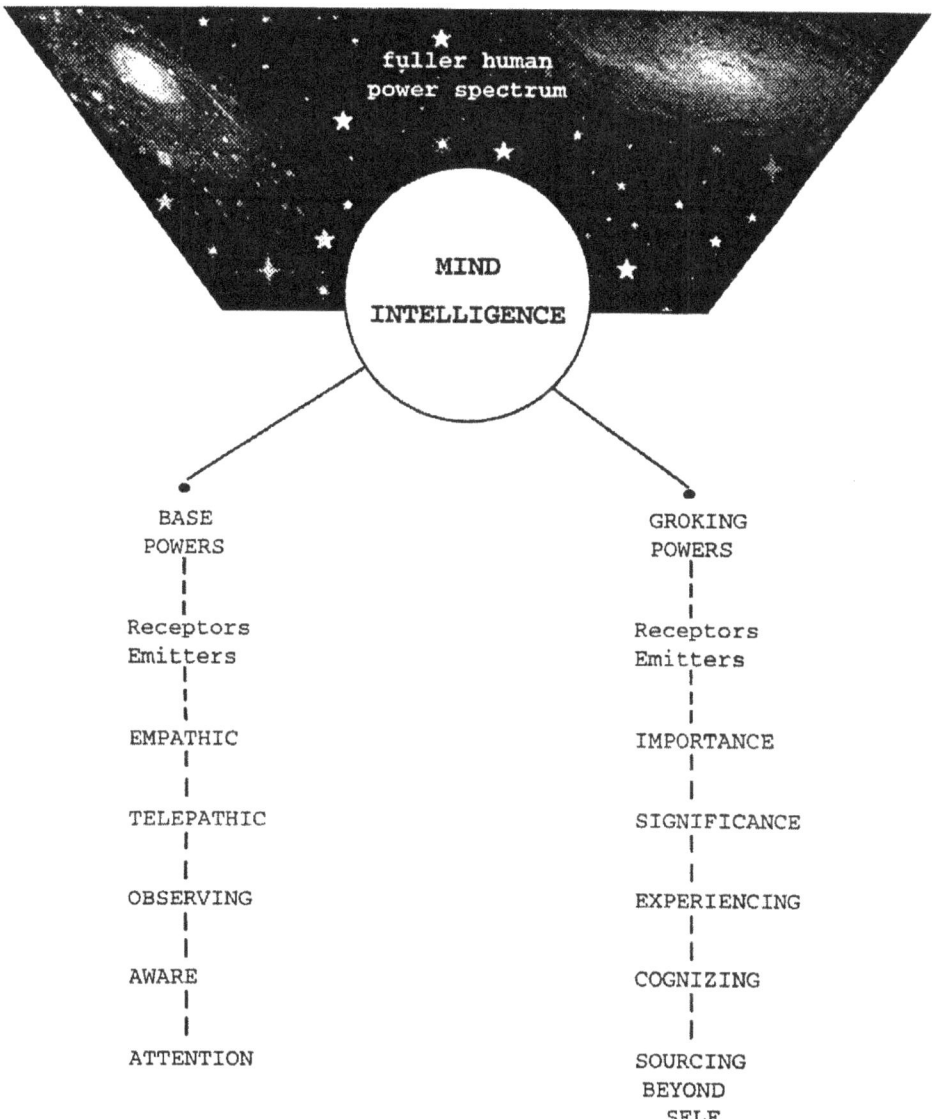

FIGURE 16. The fuller spectrum of innate human powers is probably quite extensive, but the ten powers shown above are easily recognized. These can benefit from nurturing, but can also be diminished or cut back by antagonistic non-nurturing and various elements of social conditioning. These ten powers are interactive, and can recombine into different patterns of activity.

Chapter 34

HUMAN GROKING POWERS OF SOURCING FROM BEYOND-SELF

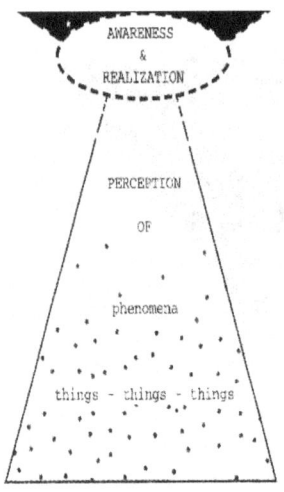

AS HAS been mentioned earlier, the English language does not contain words that might be descriptive of powers unrecognized or as yet unidentified.

This is not too much of a problem when dealing with the known and the familiar. But it becomes a difficulty when, for example, words in other languages are encountered for which there are no exact English equivalents.

For example, in India the ancient language of Sanskrit contains an abundance of words for states of awareness, consciousness, and powers of intelligence for which there are no English equivalents.

This obviously makes for various translating difficulties, and two principal ways have been used to get around them.

The most preferred way has been to select the English term that various translators think seems to be the nearest best equivalent to the Sanskrit word.

Thus, any number of Sanskrit terms have been translated in a "spiritual" context -- when in Sanskrit they refer to altered states of awareness and, sometimes, to altered states of intelligence for which there no equivalent English terms.

Sanskrit is a very flexible language, while English is not. The term SANSKRIT is composed of SAM + KAROTI, or, in English, TOGETHER + HE MAKES. Thus, in Sanskrit, words can be linked together so as to require one to grok their combined contexts.

Of all of our Western languages, German has this facility also. Any number of German terms can be linked together as one word, sometimes up to ten of them, and the Germans are quite prepared to grok the combined contexts and implications. There is even a German word for this - ZUSAMMENFASSUNG -- meaning "together fasten."

There are eight words in the heading of this chapter, and which, taken altogether, more or less bring description to a group of human powers for which there are no English terms.

HISTORICAL EVIDENCE FOR BEYOND-SELF POWERS

There does exist, however, copious historical evidence that several types of such powers do exist, and it seems that all of the types have at least two factors in common: (1) Their elements, whatever those are composed of, collectively transcend societal and cultural boundaries; and (2) The transcendental nature seems to link together all of our species in more ways than other phenomena do.

In a roundabout way, such powers also share a third factor in common. It is quite well understood that various social and societal orders do not want our species to be linked together, largely because such orders wish to be separate from one another so that they can establish their own power structures.

One way to begin discussing these powers is to cope with the "beyond-self" aspect, because this implies that there is something that has inner and outer perspectives.

Several human factors have inner and outer perspectives, but pre-eminent among them are those tiresome reality boxes that have variously been discussed earlier.

The idea that one can mentally get "boxed in" is not all that new. But the expression itself is a modern slang metaphor that refers to having one's head in a box, or to having a box around one's head -- the implied meaning being pejorative or disparaging, since it refers to limited thinking capacities.

One more serious feature of reality boxes that has been noted time and again is that they are hard to crack into, so to speak, and equally hard to crack out of.

Many can think that others might have limiting reality boxes, but that they themselves do not, having instead a good grasp of real reality.

However that matter may be resolved, what everyone does have are various information packages.

And if one can grok that real universal realities might be made up of, say, 10 billion information packages, then one can look around and also grok that most, including some of the most powerful, are perhaps best working within the contexts of only ten information packages -- or perhaps only three information packages, those of sex, money, power.

In any event, reality boxes basically consist of information packages that may or may not be too much in touch with real realities -- especially those of the universal kind.

The point being made here is that reality boxes have an "inside" and an "outside," with the added stipulation that one can "see" with respect to what is in the inside, but usually cannot "see" what is outside of the inside, so to speak.

THE TRANSCENDING NATURE OF BEYOND-SELF GROKING

It can now be suggested that if our human groking powers of beyond-self sourcing transcend anything, the first thing they must transcend involves various kinds of reality boxes. After all, if one cannot get outside of one's reality box, then any transcending processes must remain stultified.

Now, with regard to any stultifying of transcending processes, it must frankly be pointed out that most social and societal orders, and especially their power structures, cannot have individuals popping out of their reality boxes.

In fact, if such orders are to remain intact and the same, all reality boxes within them must stay the same, at least more or less so.

So any popping out of reality boxes is viewed with utmost concern and worry, and much social care is taken to ensure that information and knowledge about popping out is made unavailable, or at least is discredited in quite heartless and sometimes obscene ways.

So now the question can arise as to whether popping out from this or that reality box has any real virtues.

There is one realm of human activity where popping out of reality boxes, conventional or otherwise, is in fact admitted as a virtue: the realm of DISCOVERY.

Indeed, it is quite well understood that popping out permits discovery of this or that which has not been discovered before because of fixed reality boxes that have prevented it.

It is the case that discovery is sometimes made by "chance," or via logical deduction, but the reality boxes of the discoverer still need to recognize what "chance" or logic has made available. It is also well known that many pass over discovery because their reality boxes have prevented notice of it.

Even so, it must be pointed, out that discovery is usually considered as discovery only if it turns out that wealth and/or power can be generated and accrued from it.

There are several good histories of discovery that are available, and some even contain essays about the so-called "discovery process" in which the terms "inspiration" and "inspired" make their frequent appearance.

A discoverer (or an inventor) is usually considered as the "generative source" of whatever was discovered or invented.

It is this phrase that puts us well into the vicinity of human groking powers of beyond self-sourcing, and which makes it clear that transcending of reality boxes is not only required, but also possible, and even probable.

SOURCE - SOURCING – GENERATE

SOURCE, of course, is defined as "to rise and spring forth; a fount; a point or origin; a generative force."

The powers of sourcing thus refer to what arises or springs forth not only from within, but from outside of ourselves, and which portrays or gives direct evidence of some kind of generative force.

GENERATE (and GENERATIVE) are conceptually defined as "to bring or bringing into existence." Although this concept is referred to all of the time, almost nothing is understood about how or what is involved.

To get a larger idea about our sourcing powers, it is necessary to establish that although they may interact with other powers, they are NOT altogether dependent upon what one has already experienced or learned, or upon pre-established knowledge packages and reality boxes.

Rather, descriptions of sourcing powers are more appropriately linked to the definitions of INSPIRE and INSPIRATION:

> to influence, move, or guide by divine or supernatural causes;
> to exert an animating, enlivening, or exalting influence upon;
> the act or power of moving the intellect or emotions.

While it is commonly accepted that the source of inspired events is outside of self, it can be pointed out that the distinctions between inside and outside of self are not cast in concrete -- at least at the levels of altered states of awareness.

Indeed, as is generally accepted today, there are different, and altered states of consciousness in which such boundaries do not exist.

Although akin to inspired activity, sourcing powers more clearly belong to the innate power packages individuals are born with -- before they undergo knowledge and information adapting in conformity with pre-set societal reality boxes.

CONCEPTS THAT DISTORT BEYOND-SELF GROKING

There are at least three factors that stand in the way of groking beyond-self groking.

First, information "arriving" from inspired sources is usually thought of as some kind of metaphysical phenomenon, and it is commonly thought that only philosophers or metaphysicians are capable of thinking along such lines.

META means "beyond, or above." It can just as well mean "in addition to." It is quite clear that physicality does exist, but it is commonly understood that other stuff exists in addition to physicality.

For example, MIND -- which certainly cannot be thought of as altogether and only physical.

Second, there is the assumed reality that everything that emerges from the individual comes from some "inner" mechanisms, or from inner sourcing.

It is, after all, generally thought, in modernist times anyway, that the individual is intrinsically separate and distinct from all others, and from all else for that matter.

Even so, such stuff as social conditioning and mind programming come from sources external to the discrete and separate individual.

Third, there is the matter of "consciousness," and of altered states of it, and which individuals can, under certain circumstances, become conscious of -- but, on average, which most cannot achieve except under extraordinary circumstances.

However, in better reality, one cannot become conscious of anything unless one first becomes aware of it. So, it is more practical to think in terms of altered states of awareness -- providing one's reality boxes can permit them.

Many who experience sensing something beyond their reality boxes tend to think they have had a "mystical" experience -- or, in more modern psychological times, think they have merely gone bonkers.

HUMAN POWERS THAT SUPPORT & ENHANCE BEYOND-SELF GROKING

As it is, however, there are numerous human phenomena that could not exist if human beyond-self powers did not -- our empathic, telepathic, intuitive, and foreseeing powers, for example, and which are obviously oriented toward beyond-self sensing, experiencing, and groking.

There must be very many kinds, or states, of beyond-self groking. One such top-of-the-line state might be thought of as "cosmic consciousness," or, rather, "cosmic awareness."

The functions of such high-sounding phrases are to intimate connectivity to all that is, including the tangible and intangible, and also, perhaps, including connecting up to one's fuller spectrum of powers.

It is through energizing connectivity that one achieves various kinds of empowerment -- and even power. After, if one dwells in dis-connectivity, so to speak, dwells detached from experiencing empowerment energies, then it is difficult to conceptualize what empowerment might consist of.

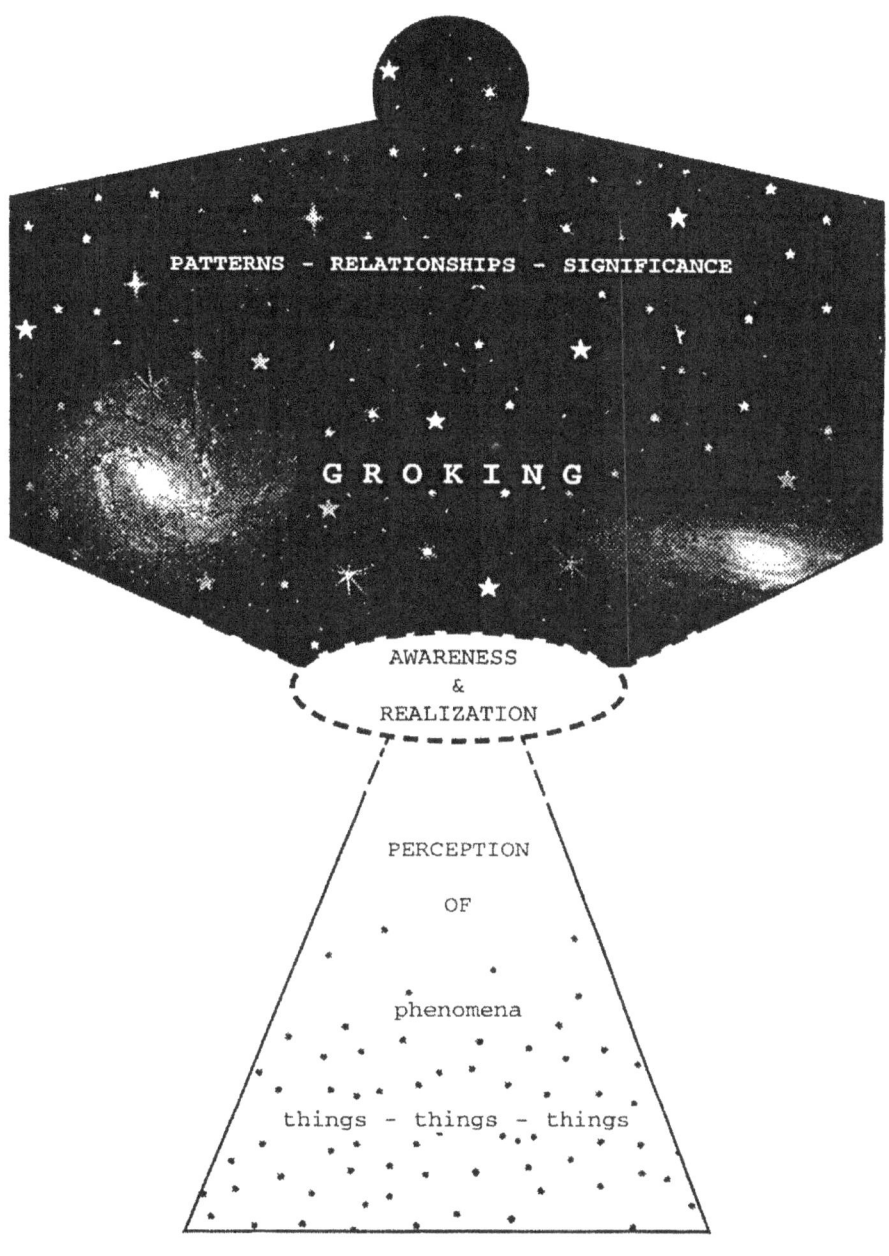

FIGURE 17. It is quite probable that groking is what it is at any given time, and so not much effort should be made to describe it in strict concrete terms. But it is clear that groking deals with patterns, relationships, and significance, usually those kinds more intangible, while perception deals with things more tangible and deductions that can be made from them.

A BIOMIND SUPERPOWERS BOOK FROM
SWANN-RYDER PRODUCTIONS, LLC

www.ingoswann.com

OTHER BOOKS BY INGO SWANN

Everybody's Guide to Natural ESP
Master of Harmlessness
Penetration
Penetration: Special Edition Updated
Preserving the Psychic Child
Psychic Literacy
Psychic Sexuality
Purple Fables
Reality Boxes
Resurrecting the Mysterious
Secrets of Power, Volume 1
Star Fire
The Great Apparitions of Mary
The Windy Song
The Wisdom Category
Your Nostradamus Factor

www.ingramcontent.com/pod-product-compliance
Lightning Source LLC
Chambersburg PA
CBHW081721100526

44591CB00016B/2457